MANAGING ENVIRONMENTAL RISK THROUGH INSURANCE

Studies in Risk and Uncertainty

edited by W. Kip Viscusi
Harvard Law School
Cambridge, MA 02138

Previously published books in the series:

Luken, R.: ENVIRONMENTAL REGULATION:
TECHNOLOGY, AMBIENT AND BENEFITS-BASED
APPROACHES

Shubik, M.: RISK, ORGANIZATIONS AND SOCIETY

Edwards, W.: UTILITY THEORIES: MEASUREMENTS AND
APPLICATIONS

Martin, W.: ENVIRONMENTAL ECONOMICS AND THE
MINING INDUSTRY

Kunreuther, H. and Easterling, D.: THE DILEMMA OF A
SITING OF HIGH-LEVEL NUCLEAR WASTE
REPOSITORY

Kniesner, T. and Leeth, J.: SIMULATING WORKPLACE
SAFETY POLICY

Christe, N.G.S. and Soguel, N.C.: CONTINGENT VALUATION,
TRANSPORT SAFETY

Battigalli, P., Montesano, A. and Panunzi, F.: DECISIONS,
GAMES AND MARKETS

MANAGING ENVIRONMENTAL RISK THROUGH INSURANCE

by

Paul K. Freeman
Eric Group, Inc.

and

Howard Kunreuther
University of Pennsylvania

KLUWER ACADEMIC PUBLISHERS
BOSTON/DORDRECHT/LONDON

Distributors for North America:
Kluwer Academic Publishers
101 Philip Drive
Assinippi Park
Norwell, Massachusetts 02061 USA

Distributors for all other countries:
Kluwer Academic Publishers Group
Distribution Centre
Post Office Box 322
3300 AH Dordrecht, THE NETHERLANDS

Library of Congress Cataloging-in-Publication Data

Freeman, Paul K.
    Managing environmental risk through insurance / Paul K. Freeman, Howard
Kunreuther.
        p. cm. — (Studies in risk and uncertainty)
    ISBN 0–7923–9901–3. — ISBN 0–8447–4019–5(pbk. : American Enterprise
Institute)
    1. Insurance, Pollution liability. 2. Liability for environmental damages.
3. Hazardous substances—Management. 4. Risk (Insurance) I. Kunreuther,
Howard. II. Title. III. Series.
HG9994.15.F74   1997
368.5′63–dc21   97-8898
                                                                                    CIP

ISBN 978-0-8447-4019-5

Copyright © 1997 by Kluwer Academic Publishers

TABLE OF CONTENTS

PREFACE

Since 1987, the ERIC Group, Inc. has been involved in the development of environmental insurance coverages for specifically identifiable exposures. Of particular interest have been the risks associated with the removal of material containing asbestos and the liability imposed on property owners by Federal and state legislation for pre-existing contamination on their property. While exploring the requirements for creating environmental insurance products, ERIC was drawn to the work at the Risk Management and Decision Processes Center (RMDPC) at the Wharton School of the University of Pennsylvania. Since 1990, ERIC and the RMDPC have worked together to explore theoretical and applied issues involved in issues of insurability.

Much of the impetus for this study came from a sabbatical from the University of Pennsylvania that Howard Kunreuther took with the ERIC group in 192–1993 which enabled the two of us to work together in a way that would have been impossible otherwise. Several interesting phenomena were uncovered as a result of this joint effort. None was more revealing than the critical role that well-specified standards play in the success of environmental insurance products. These well-specified standards are often based on regulatory policies developed at the federal level and implemented by states and municipalities. If insurance companies monitor these standards as part of their loss control activities they are, in effect, enforcing governmental environmental policy. Furthermore, as contractual instruments, environmental insurance is efficiently performing tasks historically identified with the tort system, i.e., compensating victims and deterring undesirable behavior.

Based on this finding, a logical question presents itself: can insurance be used as a means to obtain compliance with governmental environmental policy? If so, what pre-conditions must exist for insurance to play such a role? What justifications exist to undertake the effort to implement any policy based on insurance? Answering these questions requires examination of a broad mosaic of academic issues, including current systems available for providing compensation and deterrence, use of contracts (including insurance) as substitutes for tort law, limitations of regulatory policy-making by government agencies, pre-conditions for creation of insurance products and market mechanisms necessary for insurance to be purchased or sold.

The purpose of this book is to highlight the potential role that insurance and performance standards can play in managing environmental risk. It is our belief that insurance can play a significant role in dealing with one of the most problematic issues facing society today—how to compensate for environmental exposures.

—Paul K. Freeman
—Howard C. Kunreuther

FOREWORD

This careful and straightforward analysis explains how insurance can be employed to cope with risks that, in the modern environment, otherwise typically are controlled by government regulation.

The author's thesis proceeds in two basic steps. The first step is that, as a general proposition, estimation of risk can be made more rationally and therefore more efficiently by a private decision-making process than decision-making in a government regulatory scheme. This step seems hardly contestable, assuming that the private decision-maker does not have leeway to "shirk," that is, to lay off on others the consequences of errors in its calculations. If a private decision-maker cannot shirk, then it has to encapsulate unto itself the costs of undertaking the risk. Government regulators, in contrast, usually can pass on real costs to some other agency, or to some future agency personnel, or to some future cost-bearer—typically, the taxpayers. Everyone has an incentive to shirk, so that the question is not one of relative personal virtue of private and public decision-makers. Rather, it s a question of the incentive structure in which the decision-maker is enmeshed. Government decision-makers through law and regulations can impose accountability on a private agency, whereas government decision-makers often have very great difficulty making "the government" (i.e., the people in the next office) effectively accountable.

The second step in the analysis is that the costs involved in risks can be amortized or liquidated through insurance. The logic here again is simple: If a cost is likely to occur in connection with an activity, or even certain to occur, it can be covered by prepayments as well as payments after the cost is incurred. Prepayments are the insurance premiums.

Here again insurance has a distinctive virtue: The cost is covered through premiums paid in advance of the eventuality, or at least concurrently, rather than after the eventuality has occurred. Put differently, insurance involves an element of saving against the rainy day instead of waiting until the flood has occurred.

Vivid examples abound of the shortcomings of government efforts to deal with risks. The shortcomings are not avoided by calling the government programs "insurance." Witness Social Security, Medicare and the hurricane insurance provided through government subsidy for coastal dwellings.

Thus, as the authors demonstrate, there are profound virtues in trying to deal with various risks through the mechanism of private insurance instead of the mechanism of direct government regulation. Their analysis identifies and develops the nature and mechanics of these virtues.

However, the analysis presupposes characteristics of the social and political system in which an insurance scheme can operate. The key characteristic is a scheme of government regulation that will effectively prevent shirking on the part of private entities that have assumed to deal with the risks. The "regulations" contained in traditional law are as much a scheme of regulation as is direct governmental control, but are much less visible.

The relevant regulations necessary to sustain a scheme of insurance are found in traditional law: The law of contracts whereby insurance companies that have underwritten a risk can be made to pay on the coverage if the risk eventuates; the same law of contracts that gives the insured, and investors in the insured, confidence that the insurance companies will indeed be made to pay if the risk eventuates; the same law of contracts that gives the insurance companies confidence that they will be required to pay only for the risks that they have fairly assumed in their insurance coverages; and a law of torts that imposes reasonable and foreseeable awards to claimants which in turn eventuate coverage.

Traditional law—the law of contracts, property and tort—is articulated mostly by the courts, with occasional interventions by legislatures. Traditional law is enforced almost entirely through the courts and through settlement negotiations that are predicated on what the courts will do if settlement does not materialize. Hence, traditional law is essential to a "level playing field" necessary for the functioning of an insurance scheme—or indeed any system f private ordering. Society could even settle for less than a level playing field, but one only somewhat tilted and scarred with potholes.

The authors' study demonstrates the possibilities of insurance in place of government regulation. It also necessarily implies the continuing need for traditional kinds of regulation to make the "insurance solution" a workable one. Perhaps further research, building on this useful base, can identify our needs in that domain.

—Geoffrey C. Hazard, Jr.
    Director, American Law Institute

ACKNOWLEDGMENTS

During the six years that it has taken for this study to be completed, we have received considerable assistance from a number of individuals. At the ERIC group, Alan Potter and Steve Hargreaves developed the risk models for the asbestos and property transfer coverage, former Vice President of Marketing Mary Ellen Gallagher offered helpful advice on the content and structure of the book, Denise O'Meara and Eric Blommel provided administrative and research support, while Greg Chamberlin and Fred Freeman had useful inputs on the experience in marketing these new insurance products to customers.

We want to acknowledge the support of all the employees at ERIC for their support throughout the process of producing this book. A special note of appreciation to all the brokers and purchasers of environmental insurance, who helped ERIC launch its products and were willing to experiment with new ways of responding to environmental risks. Their experience provides the ingredients for the case studies presented in the book.

At the University of Pennsylvania we received helpful comments from the faculty and students associated with the Wharton Risk Management and Decision Processes Center. Special thanks go to Jon Baron, Edward Bowman, Jim Boyd, Colin Camerer, Karen Chinander, Neil Doherty, Jwee Ping Er, Jack Hershey, Eric Johnson, Paul Kleindorfer, Jacqueline Meszaros, Patrick McNulty, Eric Orts, Isadore Rosenthal, and John Villani for the many helpful discussions on how insurance in conjunction with other policy tools can improve the management of low probability-high consequence events. We greatly appreciate the administrative efforts of Anne Stamer over the past four years. Partial support for the study came from grants from the National Science Foundation to the University of Pennsylvania (Grant # SES 88-90299 and NSF Grant # 524603).

A number of individuals provided useful comments and suggestions on earlier drafts of the book which enabled us to more clearly understand what insurance can and cannot do in managing environmental risks. We wish to thank Kenneth Abraham (University of Virginia); Andrew Barnard (Transatlantic Reinsurance Co.); Ken Berger (Zurich-american Specialties); Steve Bray (University of Pennsylvania); Richard Calvert (Commerce & Industry, Inc.); Ken Cornell (Commerce & Industry, Inc.); Connie Freeman (Environmental Safety Systems, Inc.); Robert Gunther (University of Pennsylvania; Geoffrey Hazard (University of Pennsylvania); William Kronenberg (ECS, Inc.); Stan Laskowski (U.S. Environmental Protection Agency); John Merz (University of Pennsylvania); Richard Morgenstern (U.S. Environmental Protection Agency); Jeffrey O'Connell (University of Virginia); Robert Repetto (World Resources Institute); Steven Shavell (Harvard University); W. Kip Viscusi (Harvard University); and Richard Zeckhauser (Harvazrd University). Linda Pohle of The Marketing Department, Inc., carefully edited the book and constructed the index.

A special note of thanks to Christopher deMuth of the American Enterprise Institute and Zachary Rolnik of Kluwer Academic Publishers for their interest in jointly publishing this book. Their support and encouragement for this effort are greatly appreciated.

Finally we wish to thank our families (Connie, Chris, Sarah, Rachel, Gail, Laura, Joel, David, and Michael) for their support and encouragement of this effort over the past six years. They now know more about environmental risk insurance than they ever wanted to.

—PKF
—HK

Part I

Managing Societal Risks

INTRODUCTION TO PART I: OVERVIEW OF THE PROBLEM

I. MANAGING SOCIETAL RISKS

Risk is inherent in all human activities, both personal and professional. While the number and variety of risks have grown and changed dramatically throughout history, the basics remain the same--risk of loss of life, limb, health, livelihood, or property due to predictable events, e.g., reduced income upon reaching the mandatory retirement age, or to unpredictable events, e.g., loss of life in an automobile accident.

There are some risks that individuals choose to retain, consenting to pay for any losses that result from those risks. For example, once an automobile or appliance is out of warranty, consumers must pay to repair or replace it themselves.

There are many more risks, however, that individuals and businesses do not want to retain, because the costs associated with a loss would be high enough to potentially jeopardize the individual's or business' financial security. Society has developed three principal ways of allowing individuals and businesses to transfer these risks to another party.

Government Benefit Programs

There are a wide variety of Federal, state, and local government benefit programs that provide assistance to individuals and/or businesses who suffer a loss. These include Social Security (supplementary income for disabled or older Americans), unemployment (loss of income due to layoffs, downsizing, business closings), and federal disaster assistance (coverage for property damaged in natural disasters).

Tort Liability System

The tort liability system is available to anyone who has suffered a loss and seeks compensation from one or more parties responsible for causing the risk that resulted in their loss. A consumer injured by a defective product, for example, could seek redress in the courts. Alternatively, the tort liability system may address risks to health, safety, or property through regulations enforced by administrative agencies.[1]

Private Insurance

The purchase of insurance gives consumers and businesses a way to transfer the risk of loss from a specific event to a third party, usually a private insurance company. In return for accepting the risk, the insurance company receives payment from the customer in the form of an insurance premium. Insurance policies provide coverage for damage to homes, businesses, automobiles, and other property, as well as coverage for loss of income due to disability and death. They have the added advantage of encouraging loss-reduction behavior among the insureds.

II. MANAGING ENVIRONMENTAL RISKS

The focus of this book is on managing one type of societal risk--environmental risk. We have limited consideration here to those commercial activities that may adversely impact the environment and cause human health problems, create property damage, or contaminate the soil and/or ground water. Our particular concern is on the liability to individuals and/or organizations from these negative events.[2]

Our focus is exclusively on environmental risk because this is a relatively new area of societal concern, not well managed to date. It is only within the last 30 years that society has placed environmental risk high on its agenda of concerns. As a result, effective means of managing that risk are still very much in process.

The first major attempt to create a national policy for protection of the environment was passage of the National Environmental Policy Act in 1969. The creation

---

[1] For a more detailed discussion of the role that courts and administrative agencies can play in dealing with public risk, see Gillette, Clayton P. and James E. Krier, "Risks Courts, and Agencies," *University of Pennsylvania Law Review*, 138, 1990, p. 1027.

[2] This definition is similar to the one used by Abraham in his discussion of environmental liability. See Abraham, Kenneth S., "Environmental Liability and the Limits of Insurance," *Columbia Law Review*, 88, 1988, p. 942.

of the Environmental Protection Agency (EPA) occurred one year later, in 1970.[3] Over the next decade there followed a host of legislation designed to protect the air, water, soil, and, ultimately, the health of citizens, from pollutants. (See Chapter 2 for a detailed discussion of the major pieces of this legislation.)

In response to increasing environmental concern, regulation, and to the possibility of large liability for violations, (such as penalties, fines, and lawsuits), businesses have adopted more formalized environmental management procedures. Only the largest businesses have opted to retain the risk from environmental exposure because of the enormous costs involved in cleaning up a contaminated property or in treating people exposed to carcinogenic substances.

In Part I of this book, we examine how the three means of transferring risk work for businesses interested in managing their exposures to environmental risk. While some government benefit programs exist (see Chapter 1 for a discussion of these), they are becoming a less viable option today. Whether driven by budgetary limitations or by the desire to eliminate tasks that the government is not able to perform competently, there is an extensive public policy debate on the efficacy of government in directing behavior and solving society's perceived problems.

The tort liability system has become the most common arena for addressing environmental issues. But, as Chapter 2 and 3 discuss, tort liability on its own is neither equitable nor efficient in transferring risk. In fact, money spent identifying liable parties and determining their financial responsibility exceeds money spent in addressing environmental hazards.

That leaves private insurance. A clear link exists between private insurance, the tort liability system, and government policies regulating behavior. Nevertheless, insurance is a separate institutional structure designed to assume risk, even if direct governmental policy or the tort system create the underlying risk that it assumes. When such conditions exist, the insurance acts as a tool to provide financial protection and to encourage loss prevention measures.

Insurance is effective in the instances where it operates. The past decade witnessed a significant increase in the use of insurance policies to manage certain environmental risks. For example, asbestos abatement insurance, developed in 1987, protects contractors involved in the removal of asbestos from commercial buildings. These policies protect contractors against third party claims by those who develop asbestos-related diseases. Property transfer insurance protects property owners from the costs associated with cleaning up contamination discovered on their land after they have made settlement. As these two examples illustrate, there is the potential for insurance to reduce future risks and to spread risks among those parties responsible for creating them.

Part II of this book provides a framework for evaluating the appropriate role that insurance can play in managing environmental risk. The basic premise underlying the entire discussion is that society wants to move away from government benefit

---

[3] A comprehensive discussion of the origins of the EPA is contained in Landy, Mark K., Marc J. Roberts, and Stephen R. Thomas, *The Environmental Protection Agency: Asking the Wrong Questions*, Oxford University Press, New York, 1990.

programs and costly legal battles. Our proposed solution is a more effective utilization of the private sector, specifically, of the insurance industry.

However, environmental risk must meet a set of insurability conditions before insurance companies will involve themselves in developing and marketing environmental insurance policies. Chapter 4 examines these conditions in detail, followed in Chapters 5 and 6 by a discussion of insurance coverage against asbestos risk. This example serves as a prototype for the development of additional policies to cover other types of environmental risks discussed in Chapter 7.

The concluding chapter summarizes the benefits and limitations of insurance as an alternative to the current system of dealing with environmental risk.

1

MANAGING RISK THROUGH GOVERNMENT BENEFIT PROGRAMS

I. MANAGING SOCIETAL RISKS

Federal, state, and local government, through the establishment of numerous benefit (some would say entitlement) programs, has stepped forward to accept some risks on behalf of its citizens. Taxes are the primary source of revenues to compensate those in need. In some cases, notably Social Security, revenues are at least partially provided by those who directly benefit from the program—the employees—supplemented by contributions from employers.

Other types of government benefit programs are financed by all U.S. taxpayers, regardless of whether they will benefit from the program. A classic example is federal disaster assistance, which is provided to communities that experience severe losses from natural disasters. In the past, the federal government provided liberal disaster relief to victims in these communities in the form of low interest loans and forgiveness grants.[1] Today, loans are given to those in need at interest rates that

---

[1] For example, following Hurricane Agnes in 1972 the federal government, through the Small Business Administration, provided grants of up to $5,000 to cover the first layer of losses and 1 percent 30–year loans to cover the remaining portion of the damage. See Kunreuther, Howard, *Recovery from Natural Disasters: Insurance or Federal Aid*, American Enterprise Institute, Washington, D. C., 1973.

vary between 4 and 8 percent.[2] Also, the federal government generally subsidizes 75 percent of the costs of repairing public structures and infrastructure. After Hurricane Andrew in 1992 and the Mississippi floods in 1993, however, the government covered 100 percent of the costs of damage to the public sector.[3]

The primary characteristic of government benefit programs is an emphasis on equity, or "fairness," over efficiency. Government programs generally provide similar benefits at similar costs to all recipients, often without regard to their need for benefits or ability to pay. Little attention, if any, is given to risk identification or loss reduction as a basis for specifying benefit levels. Rather than attempting to modify or encourage certain types of behavior, government programs generally accept all claimants as they are, determining only if their current status makes them eligible for benefits. The question normally asked before providing disaster relief benefits is whether the claimant resided within the designated disaster area, not whether the claimant should have avoided living or working in that region in the first place.[4]

The use of government programs to reduce societal risk is subject to the American public's ever-changing notion of fairness. If the entire financial cost of recovery from natural disasters is financed through government grants, those living in high-risk areas will benefit at the expense of those in safer regions of the country. If the public feels it is everyone's responsibility to pay for the disaster losses of a few, such disaster relief programs will be considered fair. If, on the other hand, the public feels that everyone should take responsibility for their own risks, then the subsidization of high-risk individuals by all taxpayers will be considered to be unfair.[5]

By focusing on post-event criteria, government programs have an advantage over ones requiring pre-event planning. Government programs generally have fewer issues to resolve regarding qualification for benefits and, thus, have lower administrative costs for disbursing benefits. The Social Security Administration (SSA), for example, often touts the fact that there are minimal transaction costs

---

[2] These programs may be costly to taxpayers if large numbers of loans are granted at below-market interest rates. Although such programs are more stringent than they were 20 years ago, the Small Business Administration still provides subsidized low-interest loans for individuals and businesses, with terms of up to 30 years. The interest rate may not exceed 4 or 8 percent, depending on whether the recipient has credit available elsewhere. See U. S. Congress, *Federal Disaster Assistance Report of the Senate Task Force on Funding Disaster Relief,* Washington, D. C., USGPO, 1995, p. 156.

[3] Kunreuther, Howard, "Mitigating Disaster Losses Through Insurance," *Journal of Risk and Uncertainty.* (In press).

[4] Priest, George, "The Government, the Market and the Problem of Catastrophic Loss," *The Journal of Risk and Uncertainty.*

[5] New Zealand illustrates a case where a country treated disasters as the responsibility of all property owners in the country without regard to their hazard exposure. Until recently, funds to cover losses from disasters were obtained by a compulsory levy of 5 cents per $100 of property insured on all insurance contracts with fire content in them and were administered by the government's Earthquake and War Damage Commission. The philosophy behind the Fund was that natural events were unforeseen and that where they were widespread and extraordinary, citizens ought to be helped by recourse to a central fund. The country has changed its philosophy and now places much greater responsibility for loss-sharing onto the private reinsurance industry and affected communities and individuals. See Hay, Iain, "Shaken Not Stirred: Repercussions of New Zealand's Earthquake Commission Act 1993," *New Zealand Geographer,* 50(2), p. 46–50.

involved in the disbursement of its huge pool of benefits. In general, SSA pays out as much as 93–99 cents of every dollar collected, consuming only 1–7 cents per dollar in overhead.[6]

It is important to recognize that government benefit programs are not self-funding. Generally, the amount of funds available is determined on a budgetary basis. Every program competes with the requests and needs of all other government programs for its level of support. The fact that a government program presently exists does not mean that it will always be funded without question.

II. MANAGING ENVIRONMENTAL RISKS

Government benefit programs have been created in an attempt to deal with environmental risks. State Guarantee Funds (SGFs) were established by states in response to lobbying groups, such as the Petroleum Marketers Institute, who predicted that 25 percent of the nation's service stations would go out of business due to the enactment of new regulations governing underground storage tanks. An SGF is much like other government benefit programs in that it operates by collecting taxes or other fees, redistributing these funds based on some need criteria.

Under a typical plan, a SGF is funded through flat rate taxes on gasoline sales or deliveries ranging from .1 to 2 cents per gallon. All motorists in the state, therefore, are paying for the remediation costs of those firms with tanks that leak or need upgrading. Experience shows, however, that these tax revenues alone do not provide sufficient funds to cover cleanup expenses. Other tax sources must be tapped to supplement these funds, effectively creating additional forms of cross-subsidization. As a result of competition with other programs for tax revenues, several SGF programs are severely underfunded.[7]

Since the SGF program, like most government benefit programs, relies on after the fact (*ex post*) remedies, there is another drawback. No emphasis is given to tank monitoring, inspection, or replacement—all before the fact (*ex ante*) remedies that could reduce the ultimate damage and cost to society from this environmental risk.

Another program that is partially funded by all taxpayers is the Comprehensive Environmental Response, Compensation, and Liability Act (CERCLA), commonly referred to as Superfund.[8] If the federal government taxes everyone to pay for cleaning up hazardous waste sites, it is equivalent to saying that all citizens, not just those who create the pollution, must pay to remedy that pollution. Today, government regulations, and court interpretations of those regulations, hold industrial concerns responsible for cleaning up sites classified as potentially hazardous by the

---

[6] See Bernstein, Merton C., and Joan Brodshaug Bernstein, *Social Security: The System That Works*, Basic Books, Inc., New York, 1988, p. 13., and in particular, reference number 3 which cites a United States Senate report.

[7] Boyd, James and Howard Kunreuther, "Retroactive Liability and Future Risk: The Optimal Regulation of Underground Storage Tanks," *Wharton Risk Management and Decision Processes Center Working Paper*, Wharton School, University of Pennsylvania, Philadelphia, PA, September 1995.

[8] 42 U. S. C. sections 9601–9675

United States Environmental Protection Agency (EPA) or relevant state environmental agencies. However, if the parties responsible for the pollution are no longer in business or insolvent, the costs of cleanup are paid from a Trust fund, which is funded, in part, by taxpayers.[9]

III. SUMMARY

Government benefit programs play a role in managing societal risk, including environmental risk. Their strength is that they provide benefits to individuals and businesses that suffer losses. Their greatest weaknesses are that (1) they do nothing to lower the risk and likelihood of loss, and (2) they subsidize certain individuals and businesses at the expense of all taxpayers.

---

[9] Probst, Katherine and Paul Portney, *Assigning Liability for Superfund Cleanups: An Analysis of Options*, Resources for the Future, Washington, D.C., June 1992.

2

MANAGING RISK THROUGH
THE LEGAL SYSTEM

I. MANAGING SOCIETAL RISKS

The legal system transfers risk involuntarily from one party to another through a system of liability rules. Consumers take manufacturers to court for selling defective products; patients sue doctors for malpractice; accident victims often search for several parties, each of whom the victim holds partially responsible for injuries.

Tort law is the body of common law that deals with wrongs committed between parties outside of contractual obligations. The two functions of tort law are (1) to provide the basis for recovery for an injured party, and, (2) to deter others from engaging in similar activities.[1]

A tort action historically has required proof of a defendant's intentional or negligent acts before permitting recovery.[2] Plaintiffs, therefore, have had to prove the following in order to recover damages, which generally consist of bodily injury or property damage claims:

---

[1] In their treatise on torts, Prosser and Keeton note: The concern with preventing future harm has been quite important in the field of torts. The courts focus not only on compensating the victim also on with admonishing the wrongdoer. When the decisions of the court become known, and potential defendants realize that they may be held liable in the future, there is, of course, a strong incentive to prevent the occurrence of the harm. Not infrequently, one reason to impose liability is for the deliberate purpose of providing that incentive. Keeton, W., et al., *Prosser and Keeton on the Law of Torts*, section 92, 5th edition, 1984, p. 665.

[2] Prosser, William L. and John W. Wade, *Torts: Cases and Materials*, Foundation Press, 1971.

1. That a duty was owed the plaintiff by the defendant;

2. The duty was violated by the intentional or negligent acts of the defendant, which fall below a standard of care defined;

3. The acts of the defendant were the "cause" of injuries suffered by the plaintiff; and

4. The damages suffered by the plaintiff are measurable.

Once a duty exists, the standard of care governing the behavior of the defendant becomes defined. The plaintiff ordinarily must prove that the defendant violated that standard of care.

Tort law, however, is constantly evolving. Over the past 40 years, an emerging development in tort law has been the concept of enterprise liability. Enterprise liability removes the requirement that a plaintiff prove negligence when a defendant engages in particular types of activity. Instead, it imposes strict liability on a defendant engaged in those activities irrespective of a showing of negligence. In other words, if the plaintiff can show merely that the defendant's dangerous activities caused him or her to suffer any losses, then the defendant will be held liable for these losses.

Enterprise liability has emerged as the tort theory applicable to product liability claims.[3] One reason for this development is the argument made by legal scholars, and subsequently adopted by the courts, that manufacturers could police their products through quality control much more easily than consumers could determine whether products were safe.[4] Even more importantly, scholars based enterprise liability on the premise that manufacturers would want to invest in cost-effective loss prevention activities. In other words, they would adopt mitigation or prevention measures whenever the costs would be less than or equal to the benefits derived from reducing the potential losses of litigation.[5]

The view that risk should be spread across the entire population motivated these legal developments. By making manufacturers strictly liable for losses caused by their products or operations, manufacturers could include the cost of this liability in the selling prices they charged. Then, instead of claimants needing to prove negligence, funds accumulated as a result of this liability would be available for any claimant establishing that a product caused injury, regardless of the negligence of the manufacturer. In many ways, scholars expected the tort system, through strict liability, to play the role that traditional insurance plays—spreading risk across a

---

[3] Priest, George L., "The Invention of Enterprise Liability: A Critical History of the Intellectual Foundations of Modern Tort Law," *Journal of Legal Studies*, 14, 1985. p. 461–528.

[4] Shavell, Steven, *The Economics of Accident Law*, Harvard University Press, Cambridge, MA, 1987

[5] For two excellent summaries of this literature, see William Landes and Richard Posner, *The Economic Structure of Tort Law*, Harvard University Press, Cambridge, MA, 1987; and Shavell, Steven, *Economic Analysis of Accident Law*, Harvard University Press, Cambridge, MA, 1987.

population subject to a particular hazard and encouraging loss prevention measures.[6]

II. MANAGING ENVIRONMENTAL RISKS

The financial implications of environmental liability are enormous. Accrued liability for environmental risks related to real property are estimated at U. S. $2 trillion,
16 to 20 percent of the total value of all property in the United States.[7] Risk management expert H. Felix Kloman identifies environmental liability as the "risk of
the decade" for corporate risk managers in his periodical Risk Management Reports.[8]

Environmental liabilities imposed by relatively recent standards of care come
primarily from government regulation, the most frequently used method of setting
standards of care for environmental liabilities in the U. S. In the United States, a
social conscience concerning the environment has been evolving since the 1960s. It
is an evolution marked by a significant shift in viewpoint. Instead of continuing to
see the environment as a resource for economic gain, Americans are increasingly
coming to see the environment as a resource with economic and social values in its
own right. Hundreds of federal, state, and local statutes enacted in a relatively short
period of time protect those values by assigning liability for environmental contamination of the air, water, and soil resources of the United States—and by stipu-
lating who will pay for the cleanup of this contamination. The burden of this
liability is falling largely on the shoulders of the private sector, specifically on property owners.

The remainder of this chapter provides an overview of the emergence of regula-
tion-created environmental risks, details the standards of care established to impose
liability for these defined risks, and reviews the costs associated with using the court
system to impose involuntary liability for environmental risk.

Environmental Legislation in the United States

The best reflection of the seriousness with which a society views particular issues is
in the tools it is willing to give its government to deal with those issues. In the environmental realm, the U. S. government possesses extraordinary powers—powers
affecting virtually every U. S. business, not only those involved in pollution-causing
activities.

---

[6] Landes, William, and Richard Posner, *The Economic Structure of Tort Law*, Harvard University Press,
Cambridge, MA, 1987.
[7] Wilson, Albert R., *Environmental Risk: Identification and Management*, Lewis Publishers, Chelsea,
MI, 1991, p. vii.
[8] Kloman, H. Felix., "Issues for 1995," *Risk Management Reports*, Seawrack Press, Inc., Lyme, CT,
22(1), January 1995, p. 4.

As a result, the environment is subject to significant government direction about acceptable standards of behavior. In addition, that direction is frequently revised. While regulation defines acceptable behavior, court interpretation also dramatically influences the legal structure under which liability may be imposed. As a result, the process of identifying and evaluating potential environmental risk is an extraordinarily difficult task.

The Early Environmental Movement and the Environmental Protection Agency

The post-World War II years gave rise to a new political constituency in the U. S.: one that was younger, more secure financially, and better educated than its predecessors. As this generation grew in wealth, leisure time, and knowledge of the world around them, its members became more interested in the natural world and in the effects of economic development on that world. This American generation was the first to concern itself with "quality of life" as well as with "bread and butter" issues.[9] This generation brought concern for the environment into the political arena and supported legislation to protect the environment.

In response to the rise of this new constituency, Congress began to implement significant water and air quality statutes in the 1960s. In 1970, President Nixon created the U. S. Environmental Protection Agency (EPA) by Executive Order. For the first time in U. S. history, a separate agency, reporting directly to the President of the United States, became charged with environmental protection. In the mid-1970s, the EPA defined its role as the protector of public health by assuring a clean environment.[10]

Clean Water

The Clean Water Act was one of the early pieces of environmental regulation enacted in the United States. Adopted in 1972, and amended a dozen times since then, the Act was designed by legislators to protect the quality of surface water by implementing a permit system to govern the amount of contaminants discharged into the nation's waterways. Businesses must comply with discharge limits based on the "Best Practicable Control Technology Currently Available." Basically, then, the purpose of this Act is to keep water clean, and to give already polluted water a chance to become cleaner by reducing the amount of pollutants discharged into it.

---

[9] Landy, Marc K., Marc J. Roberts, and Stephen R. Thomas, *The Environmental Protection Agency: Asking The Wrong Questions*, Oxford University Press, New York, 1990, p. 22.
[10] Ibid., p. 42.

Clean Air

U. S. air pollution control legislation dates as far back as 1955. However, the Clean Air Act (when enacted in 1977) provided the most significant air quality legislation for its time. Some of the justifications for this Act include:

1. The biggest part of the nation's population is located in rapidly expanding metropolitan areas that generally cross the boundary lines of state and local jurisdictions;

2. Growth in the amount of air pollution brought about by urbanization, industrial development, and increasing use of motor vehicles results in mounting dangers to public health, agriculture, and property;

3. Prevention and control of air pollution at its source is primarily the responsibility of state and local government; and

4. Federal financial assistance and leadership is essential for the development of cooperative federal, state, regional, and local programs to prevent and control air pollution. In other words, ensuring clean air is the appropriate responsibility of the federal government.

The 1977 Clean Air Act set air quality standards for specific types of pollutants based on scientific and technical criteria. As in the Clean Water Act, the environmental protection strategy here is technologically driven by setting specific limits on amounts of discharge. It is geared towards making air cleaner and keeping it clean. The basic assumption behind its provisions is that pollution does not stay in the air, but dissipates over time.[11] Significant amendment of the Clean Air Act occurred in 1990.[12] Changes include requirements to reduce sulfur dioxide emissions (to reduce acid rain), to use reformulated (oxygenated) gasoline under certain conditions, and to require permitting for facilities using and storing threshold amounts of hazardous materials that might pose a severe risk to their surrounding communities. In addition, chemical facilities were required to develop risk management programs for dealing with substances that could create major accidents and to share these plans with the public.

Clean Soil

Environmental regulations concerning toxic substances in the soil rely upon an entirely different set of assumptions and goals than the regulations concerning air and water-polluting substances. First of all, soil retains pollution. Clean up of the soil

---

[11] Rothenberg, Eric B. and Dean Jeffrey Telego, *Environmental Risk Management: A Desk Reference*, RTM Communications, Inc., Alexandria, VA, 1991, pp. 5–10.

[12] 42 U. S. C. Sections 7401–7642.

requires physical removal of the contaminants. Someone has to pay for that removal. Who is liable for that cost? Three major pieces of U. S. regulation assign this liability:

1. Resource Conservation and Recovery Act (RCRA)

Enacted in 1976, legislators designed RCRA to protect the environment, conserve natural resources, and provide "cradle to grave" legislation governing the handling of hazardous waste.[13] Its provisions also prohibit open dumping and facilitate the conversion of existing open dumps to facilities that pose no danger to the environment or to public health. The liability imposed by RCRA applies primarily to companies that deal with hazardous materials in the normal course of their business.

2. Comprehensive Environmental Response, Compensation, and Liability Act (CERCLA)

Four years after the passage of RCRA, the United States Congress passed this Act to address the environmental problems they felt RCRA did not adequately address, specifically, problems created by hazardous waste produced and abandoned in the past. CERCLA gives the government, through the EPA, authorization to undertake emergency cleanup measures if the threat from hazardous substances presents "an imminent and substantial danger to the public health or welfare." CERCLA was reauthorized in 1986 as the Superfund Amendments and Reauthorization Act of 1986 (SARA).[14] Further amendment is currently under consideration in Congress.

CERCLA is commonly referred to as "Superfund." Superfund is, technically, the name of a hazardous substance trust fund created under CERCLA that enables the EPA to finance the immediate cleanup of abandoned hazardous waste dump sites when the liable parties are unable or unavailable to pay the costs of cleanup.

CERCLA mandates a strong liability scheme that dictates that those responsible for environmental contamination will, to the extent possible, pay the costs of cleanup. The courts have interpreted CERCLA as imposing a system of broad liability of three types:

1. Joint and several liability

    Joint and several liability imposes liability without respect to the relative proportion of liability among parties. For example, if a business is liable for any portion of a contamination, it may have liability imposed for the full cost of the environmental cleanup.

---

[13] 42 U. S. C. Sections 6901–6992k.
[14] 42 U. S. C. Sections 9601–9675.

2. Retroactive liability

Retroactive liability imposes on current owners of a property liability for all required environmental cleanups, to include prior activities performed by former owners acting lawfully at the time of the activity.

3. Strict liability

Strict liability imposes liability without a showing of criminal intent or contribution. A business can be liable for a current environmental cleanup solely because contamination now exists at unacceptable levels, even if the current owner had always complied with prior standards of behavior.

CERCLA specifies that four classes of people may be held liable for cleanup costs:

1. Current owners/operators of hazardous waste facilities.

2. Any person who formerly owned or operated a facility at the time of disposal of any hazardous substance.

3. Any person who arranged for disposal or treatment of a hazardous substance at any facility owned or operated by another person (a "generator").

4. Any transporter of hazardous waste to a facility.

In addition, the U. S. courts interpreting CERCLA have found commercial lenders to be parties liable for cleanup costs if the lender could exercise control over the environmental matters of a property, whether or not the lender actually exercised such control.

3. Underground Storage Tanks (USTs)

USTs are the most common method of petroleum storage for fuel distributors, municipalities, large firms, or any other organization that stores large amounts of fuel. There are approximately 1.4 million such tanks in the United States. The EPA estimates that the fraction of leaking tanks has been as high as 35 percent. As of 1992, there have been 185,000 confirmed releases. The estimated total cost of UST remediation is between $30 and $40 billion.[15] The EPA also estimates that a leak of one gallon of gasoline can contaminate the water supply of a city of 50,000 people. Since one-half of the U. S. population depends on groundwater for drinking water, legislators considered regulations for these tanks critical. Rules governing tanks include requirements for leak detection or inventory control and tank testing, record-keeping and reporting, corrective action, closure, and financial responsibility

---

[15] "USTs: A Busy Decade Ahead," *Environmental Times*, November, 1992, pp. 31.

for corrective action and third party liability. New tank performance standards include requirements for design, construction, installation, release detection, and compatibility.[16]

The Role of the Court System: Standards of Care and Enterprise Liability

As emerging environmental risks are identified, the government has been unwilling to assume those risks on behalf of society at large. Hence, government benefit programs are generally not part of the landscape. Rather, the government has shifted responsibility for the risks to those perceived to have created them. This is done regardless of whether the activity of the polluter was previously permissible. The phrase "polluter pays" encompasses this principle. By setting strict standards of care through regulation, the government has made the tort system the mechanism for reallocating liability.

Generally speaking, the courts have adapted enterprise liability, the tort theory applicable to product liability claims, to environmental claims.[17] Enterprise liability imposes strict liability for injuries from environmental claims and toxic chemicals. An essential requirement for recovery in an environmental claim is the establishment of a causal link between the activity of the defendant and the injury sustained by the plaintiff. This causal connection may be established several different ways. The enterprise liability doctrine, while modifying negligence standards, still requires that this causal connection be established.

The principal challenge in dealing with environmental risk is the limited scientific evidence that exists on the toxicity of most chemicals and the even more limited evidence as to their responsibility for causing diseases in individuals and injury to the environment. These limitations in the fields of toxicology and epidemiology are due to the different sensitivities between humans and animals that impair the ability to deduce human cancer risks from animal bioassays. Furthermore, the procedure of extrapolating findings from studies in which animals have far higher exposure to a risk than human beings is fraught with uncertainty.

The scientific literature on environmental risk includes lengthy debate on the inability of science to provide causal connections between environmental hazards and human illness. Toxicologists are reluctant to label more than just a few chemicals as carcinogenic and will rarely conclude that humans face a known risk simply because animals in a controlled experiment contract a disease.[18] Furthermore, there is little concrete evidence to suggest that more scientific studies and risk assessments will clarify the situation.[19]

---

[16] Rothenberg, Eric B. and Dean Jeffery Telego, *Environmental Risk Management: A Desk Reference*, RTM Communications, Inc., Alexandria, VA, 1991, pp. 151, 154.

[17] Mielenhausen, Thomas C., "Insurance Coverage for Environmental and Toxic Tort Claims," *William Mitchell Law Review,* 1991, 17, p. 945.

[18] Kraus, Nancy, T. Malmfors, and Paul Slovic, "Intuitive Toxicology: Expert and Lay Judgments of Chemical Risks," *Risk Analysis*, 1992, 12, pp. 215–232.

[19] Graham, John, Laura Green, and Marc Roberts, *In Search of Safety*, Harvard University Press, Cambridge, MA,1988.

Due to this inability to determine definite linkages between exposure and disease, there are likely to be enormous transaction costs and legal expenses incurred by companies in arguing who (if anyone) is responsible for specific losses when an individual claims injury. Even for diseases such as asbestosis (chronic lung disease) and mesothelioma (a cancer affecting the membrane lining of the chest cavity) where there is somewhat greater understanding of causality, it is often difficult for the courts to assign liability.[20]

For these reasons, the enterprise liability system causes problems for both the plaintiff, who may suffer harm from a toxic chemical or product, and the defendant, charged with responsibility for the harm. The biggest problem for plaintiffs is establishing a causal link between exposure to hazardous materials and the alleged injury or disease.[21] In some cases, failure to establish a causal link may prohibit recovery even where plaintiffs clearly establish injury. In other cases, plaintiffs may be able to collect damages, despite little connection between a toxic exposure and the occurrence of the disease.

To the extent that defendants believe that liability is being imposed on a random basis because of the lack of causal connections to their acts, it is unlikely that judgments will have the desired effect of modifying behavior. It is more likely that defendants may abandon entire areas of activity rather than produce products or services that they perceive expose them to random, high cost liability.[22]

Inefficiency of the Court System in Allocating Environmental Risk

Given the uncertainties associated with many environmental risks and the multiple parties involved, the costs of resolving environmental liability lawsuits can be extraordinarily high. Several major studies have reviewed the costs associated with using the court system as the means for imposing environmental liability. The next chapter contains a detailed comparison between the magnitude of claim payments available to claimants in tort liability cases and payments available to those who rely upon insurance to recover financially.

The transaction costs consumed by tort liability cases make it a very expensive method of collecting remediation costs. Rising litigation costs will probably increase the transaction cost percentage of total cleanup or compensation expenditures. One of the studies performed by RAND, included in our analysis, projects that litigation costs will exceed by four-fold the net compensation received by injured asbestos claimants in the coming decades.

---

[20] See Anderson, Corby, "Injury Litigation: Employer Not Liable in Case of Minimal Asbestos Exposure," *Asbestos Abatement Report*, Buraff Publications, Washington, D. C., 4(10), October 15, 1990. p. 7, and Kakalik, James S. et al., *Costs of Asbestos Litigation,* Rand Institute for Civil Justice, Santa Monica, CA, R-3042–ICJ,1983, p. 3–4.

[21] Rabin, Robert L., "Environmental Liability and the Tort System," *Houston Law Review,* 24, 1987, pp. 27; Ginsberg, William R. and Lois Weis, "Common Law Liability for Toxic Torts: A Phantom Remedy," *Hofstra Law Review*, 9, 1981, pp. 859.

[22] Huber, Peter W., *Liability: The Legal Revolution and Its Consequences.* Basic Books, New York, 1988.

III. SUMMARY

The tort system has evolved the ground rules for strict liability through the enterprise liability concept used in product liability cases. Enterprise liability eventually extended to include environmental liability. Standards of care required to assign strict liability in environmental cases have arisen through environmental legislation, regulation, or through court interpretation. The transaction costs and legal expenses incurred through the use of the court system have been substantial.

These high transaction costs suggest that alternative programs for dealing with environmental risks could improve the efficiency of delivering funds to cleanup or remediation.

In the next chapter we examine whether insurance can be a more efficient tool for allocating resources than the tort liability system.

and requiring loss prevention techniques and inspecting facilities before issuing or renewing a policy, nineteenth century insurers were able to reduce losses dramatically and provide coverage against risks for which there had previously been no protection.[6]

II. INSURANCE FEATURES

Risk Spreading

If a business bears the entire cost of losing its property to fire, the impact of such a loss on that business can be severe. If the business owns multiple properties, the damage to one facility diminishes the loss severity somewhat, because the business only loses part of its holdings. If the business pools its risk with other businesses through the purchase of fire insurance, the business can experience a further reduction in the financial impact from a fire. As a result, insurance enables activities to take place that might not otherwise occur if the business was forced to individually bear the risk associated with the activity itself.

As the above discussion illustrates, insurance spreads the economic consequences of individual events (fire) across broader groups (many businesses). In so doing, it reduces the potentially catastrophic consequences of unforeseen events on an individual or business by having those consequences absorbed by a third party. The third party, usually an insurance company, collects premiums from many to pay for the unexpected losses of a few. Insurance tends to be self-funding, with the premiums collected held in reserve to pay future claims.[7]

Variance Reduction

When insurance pools a large number of independent (uncorrelated) risks of known probability, it reduces the variance of the risk.[8] Statistically speaking, improved certainty about the likelihood and severity of loss occurs as a result of pooling a large number of such risks. Under the *law of large numbers*, the probability of each measured event (such as a loss) of a given type tends to approach the mean probability of all the aggregated events as the sample size increases. What this signifies is that a large group of entities undertaking a given risky activity can normally achieve a better estimate of the magnitude and frequency of potential losses by aggregating their risks than they can individually. The variation in frequency and severity of loss for an individual, or small group of individuals, is more difficult to estimate than for a large group.

---

[6] Ibid.

[7] Rejda, George, *Principles of Insurance*, Scott, Foresman & Co., Glenview, IL, 1982.

[8] For a more mathematically technical discussion of this phenomenon, see Priest, George L., "The Government, the Market, and the Problem of Catastrophic Loss," *Journal of Risk and Uncertainty*, 1996.

This effect of the law of large numbers makes it is possible to answer the questions "How often will drivers over 25 years of age in our metropolitan area get into an auto accident this year?" and "How much will their total repair or replacement costs be?" with greater certainty than estimating the risk for a specific driver over 25 years old.

More accurate estimates allow insurers to make more precise determinations of the reserve amounts needed to compensate for losses incurred. It is thus necessary to reserve only plus or minus 3–5 percent of the mean expected loss, for example, rather than the plus or minus 20 percent that might otherwise be required if one uses only data on individual risks.[9]

Segregation of Risks

Insurance works best when it segregates risk. This involves discriminating between different classes of potential policyholders, using such identifying features as characteristics of the individual (good drivers versus bad drivers), classes of business (trucks versus recreational automobiles), or groups with different risk exposure (general contractors versus hazardous waste removal contractors).

Segregation enables insurance providers to separate the lowest risk category (good drivers) from a risk pool (all drivers) and to separately price and sell policies to members of that category—usually at a lower premium. By so doing, it reduces cross-subsidization. Low risk insureds pay an amount based on their risk profile. Safe drivers, for example, would not be charged a rate which helps subsidize drivers with a record of accidents.

Encouraging Loss Reduction Measures

In the process of creating uniform risk categories, insurance companies have adopted techniques for modifying the behavior of potential insureds. The insurer, taking a cue from the nineteenth century mutual companies, will often require its potential policyholders to undertake specific loss reduction activities before receiving insurance coverage. In fact, insurance companies have often been the driving force behind the implementation of safety procedures. As new protective measures reduced the incidence of fire in the workplace during the nineteenth century, for example, fire risk was reduced, as were the overall costs to society.[10]

Insurance policies also offer premium reductions to individuals and businesses who have taken actions to reduce their risks or have better-than-average records regarding their past performance. Life insurance, for example, costs less for nonsmokers than for smokers. Security systems, burglarproof safes, and other loss pre-

---

[9] Hypothetical example.

[10] Bainbridge, John, *Biography of an Idea: The Story of Mutual Fire and Casualty Insurance*, Doubleday & Co., Garden City, N. Y., 1952.

vention devices lower insurance premiums.[11] Auto insurance costs less for drivers who have not had an accident in several years. Insurers design these forms of experience rating to encourage behavior that reduces overall risk exposure.

Monitoring and Control

Insurance also provides a valuable function by monitoring the activities of the insureds. Insurance providers generally undertake this monitoring function to verify that the insured operates in a manner consistent with underwriting standards. Monitoring may be as simple as verifying driving records, or as complicated as inspecting manufacturing facilities.

The insurer will not always undertake the inspection or audit itself but may hire certified inspectors or experts for this purpose. For example, after some serious accidents involving steam boilers in the nineteenth century, insurers used certified inspectors to monitor and approve boiler designs. Once these inspectors performed their work, insurers offered policies to cover any losses from a boiler explosion. The insurer knew there existed a low probability of such an event, given the certification process. In fact, the monitoring of operations by the insurance provider can have significant benefit for other parties, such as the government, interested in having the behavior of others reviewed. For nearly 100 years, operators of steam boiler vessels in the U. S. have met government regulations by securing insurance certificates for those boilers. There is discussion today of using certified third-party inspectors to monitor cold storage ammonia plants, required by an amendment to the Clean Air Act [Sec. 112(r)] to have plans in place for reducing the likelihood and costs of catastrophic accidents. Using these inspectors' reports as a guide, a newly developed insurance program could set premiums and provide coverage for a well-defined risk.[12]

III. ROLE OF REINSURANCE

Reinsurance does for the insurance company what primary insurance does for the policyholder/property owner, i.e., it provides a way to protect against unforeseen or extraordinary losses. For all but the largest insurance companies, reinsurance is almost a prerequisite to offering insurance against hazards where there is the potential for catastrophic damage. In a reinsurance contract, one insurance company (the reinsurer, or assuming insurer) charges a premium to indemnify another insur-

---

[11] Greene, Mark and James Trieschmann, *Risk and Insurance*, South-Western Publishing Co., Cincinnati, OH, 1988.

[12] Er, Jwee Ping, Howard Kunreuther, and Isadore Rosenthal, "Challenges in Utilizing Third Party Inspections for Preventing Major Chemical Accidents," Wharton School: Risk Management and Decision Processes Center Working Paper, 1996.

ance company (the ceding insurer) against all or part of the loss it may sustain under its policy or policies of insurance.

The most common type of reinsurance contract is a *treaty*, which is a broad agreement covering some portion of a particular class of business.[13] There are several types of treaties, each of which involves different sharing arrangements between the insurer and reinsurer. To illustrate these differences, consider the hypothetical case where a large fire causes $10 million in damages to a policyholder of the Accord Insurance Company. Under the terms of a *quota share treaty* arranged with the Binder Reinsurance Company, the two companies share losses equally. Both Accord and Binder pay $5 million in claims.

If the arrangement between the companies had been an *excess of loss treaty*, Accord would be responsible for all losses up to a specified amount and Binder would pay the next layer of losses up to some pre-specified maximum dollar figure. If the reinsurance contract specified $5 million in excess of $1 million, then Accord would pay the first $1 million in losses, Binder the next $5 million, and Accord would be responsible for losses exceeding $6 million—in this case, an additional $4 million.

IV. CLAIM PAYMENT CAPACITY OF TORT LIABILITY AND INSURANCE

One measure of the efficiency of any compensation program is the proportion of the total fund utilized for the payment of losses from damage claims. In the environmental arena, claims generally consist of bodily injury or remediation expenses. On the basis of data analyzing the funds expended, a major criticism of the tort liability system has been the enormous transaction costs associated with its use. By contrast, insurance generally makes available a greater percentage of funds. This advantage occurs even after taking into account the expenses associated with the interrelationship of tort liability and private insurance.

Tort Liability

Claim payment ability describes how moneys generated through the tort system (i.e., recoverable damages), through government funding, or through voluntary insurance premium payments become allocated to expense and damage claims.

Claim payment ability in tort liability cases for two areas of major, ongoing litigation—CERCLA liability and asbestos liability—provide evidence of the high transaction costs associated with this system.

Despite the distinctly different nature of the asbestos and CERCLA cases, the fund distribution associated with them prove very similar. In both cases, transaction

---

[13] A less common form of reinsurance is a facultative contract. It covers a specific risk of a ceding insurer and often is written for business that presents a significant potential for loss, such as an airplane crash.

costs have consumed approximately 60 percent of all funds generated, leaving 40 percent to be used for actual damage compensation.

This analysis of transaction costs uses studies conducted by the RAND Institute for Civil Justice,[14] as well as a study by the American Academy of Actuaries.[15] One of the RAND studies examines costs associated with CERCLA liabilities and determines the percentage commitment of total expenditures delivered to the desired end, i. e., remediating a CERCLA site. The Academy study summarizes six other CERCLA cost studies. An additional RAND study on asbestos litigation aims to discover how much of the money spent on asbestos-related bodily injury claims ended up in the hands of plaintiffs.

CERCLA Costs

The analysis begins with RAND's examination of transaction costs for CERCLA liability expenditures. RAND produced a study in 1993 which compared cleanup expenditures and transaction costs at private sector CERCLA sites. The study shows that transaction costs consume 60 percent of CERCLA site expenditures for small-to medium-sized firms.[16] The study identifies 75 percent of transaction costs as litigation expenses, with the rest consisting of either non-government approved engineering studies or other non-legal costs. The litigation costs represent legal expenses incurred in determining the level of financial responsibility of potentially responsible parties (PRPs), insurers, and/or the government.[17]

The American Academy of Actuaries also performed a review study of several Superfund cost estimates, including a Congressional Budget Office report issued April 1995. The Academy estimated that private transaction costs, not including government costs, would probably equal about 50% of the funds accumulated for CERCLA liability.[18]

---

[14] Dixon, Lloyd S., Deborah S. Drezner and James K. Hammitt, *Private Sector Cleanup Expenditures and Transaction Costs at 18 Superfund Sites*, RAND Institute for Civil Justice, Santa Monica, CA, 1993, Table 4.1, p. 30. and Kakalik, J. S., et al., *Costs of Asbestos Litigation*, RAND Institute for Civil Justice, Santa Monica, CA, 1983, Table 6.2, p. 40.

[15] Bhagavatula, Raja, et al, *Public Policy Monograph, August 1995,* "Costs Under Superfund: A Summary of Recent Studies and Comments on Reform," American Academy of Actuaries, Washington, DC, August 1995. p. 4.

[16] Dixon, Lloyd S., Deborah S. Drezner and James K. Hammitt, *Private Sector Cleanup Expenditures and Transaction Costs at 18 Superfund Sites,* RAND Institute for Civil Justice, Santa Monica, CA, 1993, Table 4.1, p. 30. Note that we used "small- to medium-sized firms" of $100 million or less in annual revenue. The figure for larger firms is approximately 32%. Using small- to medium-sized firms is more relevant to our comparison, since these firms generally purchase more insurance, as described in the *1994 Cost of Risk Survey,* Towers Perrin and the Risk and Insurance Management Society (RIMS), New York, 1994, Table 5, p. 39.

[17] Excluded are property damage and bodily injury claims made by third parties, which could considerably add to the percentages listed above. RAND excluded these figures since they are not directly related to cleanup. Note that third party property damage and bodily injury claims **are** covered under available insurance policies.

[18] Bhagavatula, Raja et al., *Public Policy Monograph, August 1995.* "Costs Under Superfund: A Summary of Recent Studies and Comments on Reform," American Academy of Actuaries, Washington, DC, August 1995. p. 4.

Table 3.1. Breakdown of Expenses for Asbestos Claims Closed as of August 26, 1982.

Item	$ Per Closed Claim	% Total Expenses + Compensation
Total Defense Expense + Compensation	$95,000	100%
Total Defense Litigation	$35,000	37%
Plaintiff Litigation Expense	$25,000	26%
Net Compensation Rec'd By Plaintiff	$35,000	37%

As shown in the RAND and Academy studies, litigation and related costs both consume a significant portion of funds accumulated to pay for CERCLA liability. Tort system costs for CERCLA liability result in up to 60% of all funds accumulated expended in transaction costs.

Asbestos Costs

Asbestos and CERCLA liabilities are distinctly different. CERCLA involves government-mandated cleanup liability. Asbestos litigation primarily involves bodily injury claims arising from exposures to asbestos fibers and resulting in various diseases, including mesothelioma, asbestosis, and lung cancer. Asbestos claims are for individual injury compensation, as opposed to payment for the remediation of environmental harm. While asbestos and CERCLA liabilities differ greatly, transaction costs associated with the use of the tort liability system to seek redress are surprisingly similar.

RAND conducted a study of the costs of asbestos litigation in order to understand the magnitude of these expenses.[19] A summary of the results of the study appears in Table 3.1, showing the expenditures of plaintiffs and defendants involved in asbestos litigation, and the allocation of those expenditures.[20] Note that 37 cents of every dollar spent on compensation actually goes to the plaintiff.

RAND scientist Deborah R. Hensler provided further support for this figure by testifying at the House Judiciary Committee hearings in October 1991, that transaction costs are 60 percent of total asbestos-related claim expenditures.[21] This figure is identical to the 60 percent figure seen in the former RAND study on CERCLA transaction-cost share for small to medium-sized firms. In both cases, only 40 percent of funds accumulated through the use of tort liability are allocated to the intended cleanup and compensation.

---

[19] Kakalik, J. S. et al., *Costs of Asbestos Litigation*, RAND Institute for Civil Justice, Santa Monica, CA, 1983.

[20] Ibid., Table 6.2, p. 40. Table 2.1 is slightly modified from Table 6.2 to focus on net compensation.

[21] Hensler, Deborah R., *Asbestos Litigation in the United States: A Brief Overview*, The RAND Institute for Civil Justice, Santa Monica, CA, P-7776–ICJ, 1991, p. 10.

Insurance

When insurance exists for specific liabilities, it has proven to be more efficient in allocating funds accumulated through the payments of premiums for their intended use.

Generally, liability insurance pays 66 percent of allocated premiums to claimants.[22] In the instances where insurers adapt insurance to very specific types of liability coverage, such as automobile insurance, the incidence of litigation is often less, and the percentage of premiums paid to claimants is even greater.[23] With respect to CERCLA liability, the insurance industry pays 58 percent of its costs per site on remediation and cleanup.[24] This represents an inverse of the tort liability claims payment ratio discussed earlier.

In each instance, the litigation expenses for the insurance companies (including their duty to defend their policy holders) remain part of the insurer's administration and underwriting costs, separate from claims paying.[25]

Conclusion

Insurance may prove to be demonstrably more efficient than the tort liability system in allocating collected funds to damage remediation or compensation. The evidence suggests that insurance may provide as much as 66 percent of collected funds for damage reimbursement, while the tort liability system provides only 40 percent of collected funds for the same purposes. Consequently, the examination of insurance as a supplemental policy tool is clearly justified on an efficiency basis.

V. SUMMARY

This chapter examined the history and features of insurance that make it a potentially powerful policy tool for reducing loss and for spreading the risk of loss among individuals and businesses that may be subject to future losses. It also examined the

---

[22] *Best's Aggregates and Averages - Property-Casualty: 1995 Edition*, A. M. Best, Oldwick, NJ, 1995, p. 175. Table is entitled "Cumulative by Line Underwriting Experience — Industry" and row item is "Other Liability."

[23] O'Connell, Jeffrey, et al, "Consumer Choice in the Auto Insurance Market," *Maryland Law Review*, 52(4), 1993, 1993, pp. 1019–1020.

[24] Levin, Alan M., CFA, "Standard & Poor's Environmental Liability Report, March 13, 1996: Environmental Liability and the Insurance Industry," *Insurance News Network*, March 13, 1996, http://www.insure.com/ratings/reports/sp_environmental.html

[25] What remains unknown from the percentage of the premium paid for claims is the amount expended in plaintiff costs. No reliable statistical information has been found on this issue. Comparisons cannot be made with plaintiff costs in pure tort liability cases, because sometimes claims are paid with little or no litigation. It might be inferred from this latter fact that plaintiff costs would be, in general, significantly less than plaintiff costs in pure tort liability cases.

important role that reinsurance plays in the process. The chapter provides evidence that transaction costs for insurance, even in the environmental arena, were much lower than under the legal system, particularly for smaller firms. On the basis of these data, insurance appears to be a promising alternative to the current practice of dealing with environmental risks solely through the tort liability system. However, for insurance to be feasible for a specific risk, it must also meet the conditions of insurability and marketability. We examine these issues in Part II.

Part II

Managing Environmental Risks

INTRODUCTION TO PART II: INSURING ENVIRONMENTAL RISKS

Part I of this book examined the roles of government benefit programs, the current legal system, and insurance in managing societal risk. It concluded that, in the area of managing environmental risk specifically, public policy makers desire fewer government programs, not more. And, it identified that the legal system currently consumes more dollars for transaction costs than it provides for compensation of plaintiffs or for cleanup of contamination. There may be opportunities to use insurance more effectively to reduce losses from environmental risk and to provide better remedial action at much lower cost.

Part I also pointed out several additional advantages that insurance has over the current management of environmental risk. First of all, insurance firms have both an incentive and the expertise to collect scientific data on the nature of a given risk in order to determine a premium. Other businesses do not normally undertake this process of risk identification to the same extent as insurers do.

Second, the insurer also has a business incentive to estimate risks more accurately through audits and inspections prior to issuing a policy.

Third, insurers can play a role in reducing the losses from environmental risks by monitoring the activities of their customers. If a contractor cleaning up asbestos knows that he has insurance protection against third-party claims from individuals who develop asbestosis, there is less incentive for him to worry about how many asbestos particles are in the air. The insurer, on the other hand, harbors a great deal of concern about the fiber content in the air and, thus, has an incentive to monitor the cleanup process.

In the following chapters we explore the role insurance can play in providing coverage against certain environmental risks. Chapter 4 discusses problems of insurability and marketability of risk.

Chapters 5 and 6 turn to the experience of developing and marketing environmental insurance products by focusing on coverage for liabilities associated with asbestos in existing facilities. Chapter 7 reviews the experiences from attempts to insure other environmental risks and identifies characteristics that either made the risks insurable or uninsurable. The final chapter reviews the benefits and limitations of insurance and identifies lessons learned from the examples tested in the marketplace.

THE NATURE OF THE INTERRELATIONSHIP BETWEEN TORT LIABILITY AND LIABILITY INSURANCE

The academic literature has focused its attention in recent years on the interrelationship of tort liability, environmental risk, and liability insurance. Kenneth S. Abraham[1] produced the most knowledgeable work in this area, relied upon extensively by the American Law Institute's (ALI) two-volume treatment of "Enterprise Liability for Personal Injury" (1991).[2]

The discussion centers on the "creation" of liability through the use of the tort system, and the "response" of the liability insurance system to the newly emerging torts. In fact, the symbiotic relationship between the tort system and liability insurance is clearly the focus of this discussion.[3]

The following chapters address the creation of insurance products for environmental risks. They address the issues associated with the concern regarding interpretation of the policy language, quantification of risk with changing, variable legal standards, the marketing of insurance considering the vagaries of liability concerns, and risk tolerances (real or imagined) of potential customers.

The following chapters describe the process by which an insurance entity attempts to create products, fully aware of the academic concerns of the proper relationship of insurance, tort liability, and environmental risks. Within the nexus of these issues, it is possible to create insurance products that may apply the benefits of insurance to this emerging arena of risk management.

It should be noted that two fundamental problems arise when testing environmental-related insurance concepts against the insurability conditions outlined in the last chapter.

---

[1] See Abraham, Kenneth S., *Environmental Liability Insurance Law: An Analysis of Toxic Tort and Hazardous Waste Insurance Coverage Issues*, Prentice-Hall, 1991.

[2] See in particular, Chapter 2, Vol. I, "Tort Law and Liability Insurance" and Chapter 11, Vol. I, "Environmental Injuries."

[3] See Syverud, Kent, "The Logic of Liability Insurance Purchases," *Texas Law Review*, 72, 1994, p. 1629.

First, the court decisions often require insurers to pay damages for losses insurance policies were never intended to cover. This is a direct result of policy coverage interpretation problems, which have intensified due to changing definitions of liability. Because of varying policy language interpretation, the determination of loss and loss limits has been arduous and the setting of rates extremely difficult. To address this problem there is a need to maintain the integrity of the policy language. Every insurance policy defines the contractual limits of coverage, establishes the Maximum Possible Loss ("MPL"), and precisely describes the insured risks. If the policy language is interpreted differently than the insurer intended, a drastic change in the original MPL may expose the insurer to losses that the premium collected (based on the original MPL) cannot cover.[4]

Secondly, statistically valid information on the probability and magnitude of loss based on historical claims experience generally does not exist in the environmental arena. Insurers, therefore, cannot calculate the potential claim component of their product using traditional actuarial techniques. Faced with these problems, most traditional insurers have chosen not to explore the environmental market.

To deal with this problem, and to specify appropriate premiums, insurers must identify the frequency of losses of different magnitudes as well as the maximum possible insured loss. Most environmental risks are a result of governmental policy, and have been classified as such only recently. Hence there is limited historical data on which to specify premiums. Therefore, insurers must find other methods of loss assessment that rely on scientific and engineering studies.

---

[4] A classic case is *Jackson Township* where the court required an insurance company to pay for groundwater contamination. The insurance policy indicated that it would cover only "sudden and accidental damage." This was interpreted by the court to mean "unexpected and unintended." The case was appealed and eventually settled out of court, but it sent a signal to the insurance industry that it had to be extraordinarily careful with policy language. For more information on the Jackson Township Case see Cheek, Leslie, "Insurability Issues Associated with Cleaning Up Inactive Hazardous Waste Sites," in Kunreuther, Howard and Rajeev Gowda, *Integrating Insurance and Risk Management for Hazardous Wastes*, Boston, MA, Kluwer Academic Publishers, Boston, 1990.

4

THE INSURABILITY AND MARKETABILITY OF RISK

While it may seem quite obvious, insurance is only a viable solution for those risks that are insurable and that yield insurance products that are marketable. What makes a risk insurable and an insurance product marketable? Insurable means that an insurance company can set a premium that accurately reflects the applicable risk. Marketable means that there must be enough individuals or businesses willing to buy coverage for the risk at a premium that covers costs and yields a profit for insurers.

The two phases of the process—determining whether the risk is insurable and whether the insurance product is marketable—are usually considered in parallel rather than sequentially. The discussion of Insurability in Section I and Marketability in Section II implies no linear order. Section III of the chapter outlines how an insurer determines what premium to set based on insurability and marketability criteria and what role reinsurance plays in making certain coverages possible.

I. TWO INSURABILITY CONDITIONS

Insurers require the fulfillment of two primary conditions before providing coverage against an uncertain event. The first condition is the ability to identify and, possibly, quantify the risk. Insurers must know that it is possible to estimate what losses they are likely to incur when providing different levels of coverage. The second condition is the ability to set premiums for each potential customer or class of customers. This requires some knowledge of the customer's risk in relation to others in the population of potential insureds.

An insurable risk satisfies both the first and second conditions, but does not guarantee a profitable line of business. If it is not possible to specify a rate where there is sufficient demand to yield sufficient profit for insurers to supply coverage, there will be no market for this type of coverage.

Condition 1: Identifying the Risk

Satisfying this condition requires estimates of (1) the frequency of specific events occurring, and (2) the magnitude of the loss should the event occur. Three examples illustrate the type of data used to identify the risk. In some cases this may enable the insured to specify a set of estimates on which to base an insurance premium. In other cases the data may be much less specific.

A. Fire

Rating agencies typically collect data on all the losses incurred over a period of time for a particular risk and an exposure unit. Suppose the hazard is fire and the exposure unit is a well-defined entity, such as a wood frame home to be insured for one year in California. The typical measurement is the pure premium (PP), given by:

$$PP = \text{Total Losses/Exposure Unit}^1 \qquad (4.1)$$

Suppose the rating agency has collected data on 100,000 wood frame homes in California and has determined that the total annual losses from fires in these types of homes over the past year is $20 million. Analysis of the collected data provides the foundation for determination of the probability and magnitude of loss that will occur. If this data is representative of the expected loss to these same 100,000 units next year, then, PP is:

$$(1) \ PP = \$20,000,000/100,000 = \$200$$

This figure is simply an average. It does not differentiate between the locations of wood frame homes in the state, the distance of each home from a fire hydrant, or the quality of the fire department serving different communities. Underwriters often take all of these factors into consideration when setting final rates. In doing so, underwriters calculate a premium that reflects the risk to particular structures.

---

[1] The pure premium normally considers loss adjustment expenses for settling a claim. We will assume that this component is part of total losses. For more details on calculating pure premiums see Launie, J., J. Lee, and N. Baglini, *Principles of Property and Liability Underwriting* (Third Edition), Insurance Institute of America, Malvern, PA, 1986.

B. Earthquakes

If there were considerable data available on annual damage to wood frame homes in California from earthquakes of different magnitudes, underwriters might use a method similar to the one described above to determine the probability and magnitude of loss. Due to the infrequency of earthquakes and the relatively few number of homes insured against the earthquake peril, however, this type of analysis is not feasible at this time. Instead, insurance providers would need to turn to scientific studies by seismologists and geologists to estimate the frequency of earthquakes of different magnitudes as well as the damage that is likely to occur to different structures from such disasters. Even then, insurers may only be able to identify the risk in a rather crude way.

Figure 4.1 (page 40) depicts the type of information required to determine the pure premium for a wood frame house subject to earthquake damage in California. The x-axis (Magnitude of Loss) would be the amount of damage an earthquake might cause to a wood frame home of a given value. The y-axis (Probability) specifies the annual probability that a wood frame home in a specific region of California would suffer a specified amount of loss from an earthquake.

If these data are available from scientific studies, the pure premium in this case would be equivalent to the expected loss (E(L)) which is given by the area under the curve in Figure 4.1.

The considerable damage data collected by seismologists and engineers since the Alaskan earthquake of 1964 has increased our understanding of the performance of various types of buildings and structures in earthquakes of different magnitudes.[2] While seismologists and geologists cannot predict with certainty the probability of earthquakes of different magnitudes occurring in specific regions of California, they can provide conservative estimates of the risk. For example, it is possible to develop a worst case scenario as shown by point *A in Figure 4.1.

Where the coordinates are the probability assigned by seismologists to the most severe earthquake they consider credible, and the engineers' best estimate of the maximum likely damage to a wood frame house from such an earthquake.

C. Underground Storage Tanks (USTs)

Suppose that an insurer wants to identify the risk and to estimate the pure premium for a new technological advance, such as an improved design for USTs. Since there are no historical data associated with the risk, the insurer would have to rely on scientific studies to estimate the probabilities (p_i) and cleanup costs (L_i) associated with a particular type of defect (i) in the tank that causes a leak.

Insofar as the insurer has some confidence in these scientific estimates of the performance of the tank and the costs of the cleanup from leaks of different magnitudes, it should be able to identify the risk. If, on the other hand, the insurer is highly uncertain about the frequency or loss estimates, it may conclude that it would

---

[2] Shah, Haresh et al., "Managing Seismic Risk," *Journal of Risk and Uncertainty*, (in press).

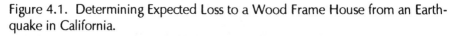

Figure 4.1. Determining Expected Loss to a Wood Frame House from an Earth-quake in California.

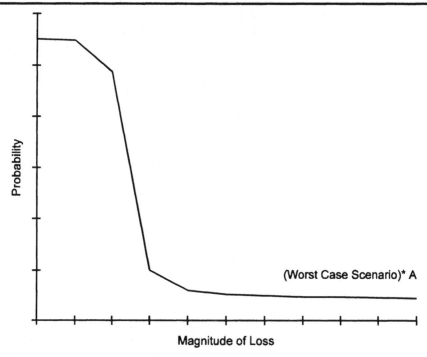

be difficult to characterize the risk with any degree of accuracy. In this case it would consider USTs an uninsurable risk.

Condition 2: Setting Premiums for Specific Risks

Once a risk is identified and, in some cases, quantified, the insurer can determine what premium must be charged in order to make a profit. There are a number of factors that come into play in determining this dollar figure.[3]

A. Ambiguity of Risk

Not surprisingly, the higher the uncertainty regarding the probability and mag-nitude of a specific loss, the higher the premium will be. As shown by a series of empirical studies, actuaries and underwriters are ambiguity-averse and risk-averse

---

[3] A comprehensive review of the theoretical literature on the impact of these factors on the pricing of in-surance and the viability of insurance markets can be found in the paper by Georges Dionne and Scott Harrington entitled "An Introduction to Insurance Economics" in Dionne, Georges and Scott Harrington, *Foundations of Insurance Economics*, Kluwer Academic Publishers, Boston, 1992, as well as in the other papers in the volume that the two authors have edited.

so that they tend to utilize worst case scenarios, as well as estimates of expected losses, in determining what premiums to set.[4]

One study mailed a questionnaire to 896 underwriters in 190 randomly chosen property and casualty insurance firms to determine the pure premiums[5] they would set for the risk of earthquake or a leaking UST. The earthquake scenario involved insuring a factory against property damage from a severe earthquake. The UST scenario involved liability coverage for owners of a tank containing toxic chemicals if the tank leaks. A neutral risk scenario acted as a reference point for the two context-based scenarios. It simply provided probability and loss estimates for an unnamed peril.

For each scenario, the questionnaire presented four cases, each reflecting the degree of ambiguity and uncertainty surrounding the probability and loss as shown in Table 4.2. A well-specified probability (p) referred to a situation in which there are considerable past data on a particular event that enable "all experts to agree that the probability of a loss is p." An ambiguous probability (Ap) refers to the case where "there is wide disagreement about the estimate of p and a high degree of uncertainty among the experts." A known loss (L) indicates that all experts agree that, if a specific event occurs, the loss will equal L. An uncertain loss (UL) refers to a situation where the experts' best estimate of a loss is L, but estimates range from L_{min} to L_{max}.

Case 1 reflects well-known risks for which large actuarial databases exist, e.g. life, automobile, and fire insurance. Satellite accidents are an example of a Case 2 risk, since there is normally considerable uncertainty regarding the chances of their occurrence. If they do happen, however, the satellite is destroyed and the loss is well-specified. Playground accidents illustrate Case 3 risk, since there are good data on the chances of an accident occurring, but considerable uncertainty as to the magnitude of the liability award should a person be injured or killed. Finally, there is considerable ambiguity and uncertainty related to earthquake and UST risks so they are appropriately classified as Case 4.

In the questionnaire to the underwriters, Case 1 was represented by providing a well-specified probability (p=.01) and a well-specified loss (L=$1 million). The other three cases introduced ambiguity and uncertainty. For example, the case where L=$1 million, the uncertain estimates were said to range from L=$0 to L=$2 million.

Forty-three insurance companies (22.6 percent of those solicited) returned one hundred seventy-one completed questionnaires (19.1 percent of the total mailed). Table 4.3 shows the average ratio of the premiums for the three cases where there is uncertainty and ambiguity in either p and/or L compared to Case 1 where both p and L are known. The data reveal that underwriters will charge a much higher premium when there is ambiguity and uncertainty regarding probabilities and/or losses.

---

[4] For more details on the survey and the analysis of findings see Kunreuther, Howard, Jacqueline Meszaros, Robin Hogarth and Mark Spranka, "Ambiguity and Underwriter Decision Processes," *Journal of Economic Behavior and Organization*, 26, 1995, pp. 337-352.

[5] The questionnaire instructions stated that pure premiums should exclude "loss adjustment expenses, claims expenses, commissions, premium taxes, defense costs, profits, investment return and the time valuation of money."

Table 4.2. Classification of Risks by Degree of Ambiguity and Uncertainty

	Known Loss	Unknown Loss
Well-Specified Probability	Case 1 p, L Life, Auto, Fire	Case 3 p, UL Playground Accidents
Ambiguous Probability	Case 2 Ap, L Satellite, New Products	Case 4 Ap, UL Earthquake, USTs

Table 4.3. Ratio of Average Pure Premiums Specified by Underwriters Relative to Well-Specified Case (Case 1) (p = .01; L = $1 million).

Scenario	p, L Case 1	Ap, L Case 2	p, UL Case 3	Ap, UL Case 4
Neutral (N = 24)	1	1.5	1.1	1.7
Earthquake (N = 23)	1	1.2	1.3	1.5
UST (N = 32)	1	1.5	1.4	1.8
N = Number of Respondents				

Source: Kunreuther, Meszaros, Hogarth and Spranken (1995)

For example, as shown in Table 4.3, the premium for the UST scenario (Case 4) was 1.8 times higher than for the well-specified Case 1 scenario.

Why do actuaries and underwriters price uncertain and ambiguous risks higher than well-specified risks? In two very insightful papers,[6] Stone describes insurer motivation in setting premiums for any particular risk. Insurers remain concerned about the impact of their actions on the stability and solvency of their firm.[7] Insurers measure stability by the loss ratio (LR), i.e., paid losses versus written premiums for a particular risk. In order to achieve stability, a probability of less than some specified level p' (e.g., p' =.05) is required, so that the loss ratio exceeds a certain target level LR* (e.g., LR*= 1).

Insurers measure solvency by the survival constraint that relates aggregate losses for the risk in question to the current surplus, plus premiums written. It requires that the probability of insolvency be less than p" (e.g. p"= 1 in 100,000). Berger and Kunreuther have shown that, if underwriters and actuaries are mindful of the two

[6] Stone, John, "A Theory of Capacity and the Insurance of Catastrophic Risks: Part I," and "... Part II," *Journal of Risk and Insurance*, 40, 1973, pp. 231-243 (Part I) and 40, 1973, pp. 339-355 (Part II).
[7] This model of underwriter behavior is consistent with recent analyses as to why insurance firms want to purchase reinsurance. For more details see Doherty, Neil and S. M. Tinic, "A Note on Reinsurance under Conditions of Capital Market Equilibrium," *Journal of Finance, Vol.* 36, 1982, pp. 949-953, and Myers, David and Clifford Smith, "On Corporate Demand for Insurance: Evidence from the Reinsurance Market," *Journal of Business*, 63, 1990, pp. 19-40.

constraints of stability and solvency, they will normally set higher premiums as specific risks become more ambiguous and uncertain.[8]

B. Adverse Selection

If the insurer cannot distinguish between the probability of loss for different risk categories, it faces the problem of adverse selection. What this means is that if the insurer sets a premium based on the average probability of a loss using the entire population as a basis for this estimate, only the poorer risks will want to purchase coverage. As a result, the insurer expects to lose money on each policy sold.

The assumption underlying adverse selection is that purchasers of insurance have an advantage—they know their *risk type*. Insurers, on the other hand, must incur considerable expense to collect information in order to distinguish between risks. A simple example illustrates the problem of adverse selection for a risk where the probabilities of a loss p_G= .1 (good risks) and p_B= .3 (bad risks). For simplicity, assume that the loss is L = $100 for both groups and that there are an equal number of potentially insurable individuals (N= 50) in each risk class. Table 4.4 summarizes the above data.

In this example, the expected loss for a random individual in the population is twenty.[9] If the insurer charged an actuarially fair premium across the entire population only the bad risk class would normally purchase coverage since their expected loss is 30 [.3(100)]. They would be delighted to pay 20 for insurance. The good risks have an expected loss of 10 [.1(100)], so any party interested in paying 20 for coverage would have to be extremely risk averse. Hence, the insurer would suffer an expected loss of -10 on every policy sold.

There are several ways that insurers can deal with this problem. If the company knows the probabilities associated with good and bad risks, but does not know the characteristics of the individuals associated with these risks, it can raise the premium to at least 30 so that it will not lose money on any individual purchasing coverage. In reality, if there is an entire spectrum of risks, the insurer may only be able to offer coverage to the worst risk class in order to make a profit. But, raising premiums is likely to produce weak market results because very few of the individuals interested in purchasing insurance to cover their risk will actually do so at the higher rate. If the estimated number of policies sold at this premium will not enable the insurer to cover its administrative and marketing expenses, and still make a profit, the insurer will not offer coverage.[10]

---

[8] Berger, Larry and Howard Kunreuther, "Safety First and Ambiguity," *Journal of Actuarial Practice*, 1995.

[9] The expected loss for a random individual in the population is calculated as follows: [50(.1)(100) + 50(.3)(100)]/100 =20.

[10] See Akerlof, George, "The Market for 'Lemons': Quality Uncertainty and the Market Mechanisms," *Quarterly Journal of Economics*, 84, 488-500 for the classic study on why changing price will not overcome the adverse selection problem.

Table 4.4. Data for Adverse Selection Example.

Good Risks	$p_G = .1$	L = 100	N = 50
Bad Risks	$p_B = .3$	L = 100	N = 50

Table 4.5. Data for Moral Hazard Example.

Before Insurance	p = .1	L = 100	N = 100
After Insurance	p = .3	L = 100	N = 100

A second way for the insurer to deal with adverse selection is to offer two differ-ent price-coverage contracts.[11] Assume that poor risks will want to purchase con-tract 1 and good risks will purchase contract 2. Thus, contract 1 could be offered at Price = 30 and Coverage = 100, while contract 2 could be Price = 10 and Coverage = 40. Since the good risks would arguably prefer contract 1 over 2 and the poor risks would arguably prefer contract 2 over 1, this would be one way for the insurers to market coverage to both groups while still breaking even.

Finally, the insurer could require some type of audit to determine the nature of the risk. In the case of property, the audit could take the form of an inspection of the structure and its contents. For individuals, it could be some type of an examination, e.g., a medical exam for health insurance. Certain types of coverage may not lend themselves to an exam, however, due to the nature of the risk. It is difficult to test a person for driving ability, for example, although past records and experience may be useful indicators of a person's risk category.

In summary, it is important to remember that the problem of adverse selection only emerges if there is information asymmetry between the persons considering the purchase of insurance and by the firms selling coverage. If the purchasers have no better information than the underwriters on their risks, then both groups are on equal footing. If this is the case, coverage could be offered at a single premium based upon the average risk. Both good and bad risks would want to purchase poli-cies at that price.

C. Moral Hazard

Providing insurance protection may serve as an incentive for a customer to be-have more carelessly than before he or she had coverage. If the insurer cannot pre-dict this behavior, and relies on past loss data from uninsured individuals to estimate rates, the resulting premium is likely to be too low to cover losses.

The moral hazard problem directly relates to the difficulty in monitoring and controlling customer behavior once insured. How do you monitor carelessness? Can

[11] This solution has been developed by Rothschild and Stiglitz. See Rothschild, Michael and Joseph Stiglitz, "Equilibrium in Competitive Insurance Markets: An Essay on the Economics of Imperfect Infor-mation," *Quarterly Journal of Economics*, 90, 1976, pp. 629-650.

you determine when a person decides to collect more on a damage claim than he or she deserves, e.g., making false reports or moving old furniture to the basement just before a flood hits the house?[12]

The example used above to illustrate adverse selection can also demonstrate moral hazard. With adverse selection, the insurer cannot distinguish between good and bad risks. Moral hazard exists because the insurer must estimate the premium based on the probability of a loss before the insurance purchase, but the actual probability of a loss may be much higher after a policy sells. Table 4.5 on the preceding page depicts these data for the case in which there are 100 individuals, each of whom face the same loss of 100. The probability of a loss, however, increases from p=.1 before insurance to p=.3 after the sale of coverage.

If the insurance company does not know moral hazard exists, it will sell policies at a price of 10 to reflect the estimated actuarial loss (.1 x 100). The expected loss, however, will be 30, since p increases to .3 after the insurance purchase. Therefore, the firm will lose -20 on each policy it sells.

One way to avoid the problem of moral hazard is to raise the premium to 30 to reflect the increase in the probability (p) that occurs after a policy sale. In this case, there will *not* be a decrease in policies sold, as there was in the adverse selection example. Those individuals willing to buy coverage at a price of 10 will still want to buy a policy at 30, since they know that their probability of a loss with insurance is .3.

Another way to avoid moral hazard is to introduce deductibles and coinsurance as part of the insurance contract. A deductible of D dollars means that the insured party must pay the first D dollars of any loss. If D is sufficiently large, there will be little incentive for the insureds to behave more carelessly than they did prior to purchasing coverage, because they must cover a significant portion of the loss themselves.

A related approach is to use coinsurance, which means the insurer and the firm share the loss together. An 80 percent coinsurance clause in an insurance policy means that the insurer pays 80 percent of the loss (above a deductible) and the insured pays the other 20 percent. As with a deductible, this type of risk-sharing encourages safer behavior, because the insureds want to avoid having to pay for some of the losses.[13]

A fourth way of encouraging safer behavior is to place upper limits on the amount of coverage an individual or enterprise can purchase. If the insurer will only provide $500,000 worth of coverage on a structure and contents worth $1 million,

---

[12] This is an example of *ex post* moral hazard where the insurer does **not** know the nature of the accident and hence cannot determine whether the damage claim is exaggerated. For a more detailed discussion of *ex post* moral hazard in the context of insurance problems, see Spence, Michael and Richard Zeckhauser, "Insurance, Information and Individual Action," *American Economic Review*, 61, 1971, pp.380-387.

[13] For more details on the role of deductibles and coinsurance in reducing the chances of moral hazard, see Pauly, Mark, "The Economics of Moral Hazard: Comment," *American Economic Review*, 58, 1968, pp. 531-536.

then the insured knows he or she will have to incur any residual costs of losses above $500,000.[14]

Even with these clauses in an insurance contract, the insureds may still behave more carelessly than they would if they did not have coverage, simply because of their protection against a large portion of the loss. For example, they may decide **not** to take precautionary measures otherwise adopted without insurance. The insured may view the cost of these measures as too high relative to the dollar benefits potentially received from this investment.

If the insurer can learn in advance the relative likelihood that an insured develops less interest in loss reduction activity after purchasing a policy, then it can charge a higher insurance premium to reflect this increased risk — or require specific protective measure(s) as a condition of insurance. In either case, the insurer overcomes moral hazard.

D. Correlated Risk

By correlated risk we mean the simultaneous occurrence of many losses from a single event. Natural disasters, such as earthquakes and floods, are illustrations of events where the losses in a community are highly correlated; many homes in the affected area may be damaged or destroyed by a single disaster.

If insurers are concerned with the possibility of insolvency and face highly correlated risks from one event, they may want to charge a higher premium to protect themselves against the possibility of experiencing catastrophic losses. An insurer will face this problem if it has many eggs in one basket, such as mainly providing earthquake coverage to homes in Los Angeles County rather than diversifying across the entire state of California.

To illustrate the impact of correlated risks on the distribution of losses and the possibility of insolvency, assume that there are two policies sold against a risk where $p = .1$, $L = 100$ and the insurers assets are 70 prior to charging any premiums. The actuarial loss for each policy is 10. Table 4.6 on the following page depicts the probable distribution of losses for the two policies, when the losses are independent of each other and when they are perfectly correlated.[15]

The expected loss for both the correlated and uncorrelated risks is 20. However, since the variance associated with the correlated risks will always be higher than uncorrelated risks having the same expected loss, insurers concerned with insolvency will want to charge a higher premium for the correlated risk. More specifically, if the insurer charges less than 15 per risk, its total assets will be less than 200. If it experiences 2 losses during the year, it will be forced to declare insolvency. The probability of this happening will be .01 if the risks are independent and .10 if the risks are perfectly correlated.

---

[14] We are assuming that the firm will not be able to purchase a second insurance policy for $500,000 to supplement the first one and, hence, be fully protected against a loss of $1 million (except for deductibles and insurance clauses).

[15] The probabilities for the independent events were calculated as follows. L=0 occurs if neither policy suffers a loss which occurs with p=(9 X .9)= .81; L=100 occurs if either policy 1 or 2 suffers a loss which has p=(2 X .1 X .9)= .18; L=200 occurs if both policies 1 and 2 suffer losses which have p=(.1 X .1)= .01.

Table 4.6. Data for Correlated Risk Example.

Risks	L = 0	L = 100	L = 200
Independent	p = .81	p = .18	p = .01
Perfectly Correlated	p = .9		p = .1

Empirical data on the impact of correlated risks on premium-setting behavior comes from a mail survey of professional actuaries who were members of the Casualty Actuarial Society.[16] Of the 1165 individuals receiving questionnaires, 463, or 40 percent, returned valid responses. Each of the actuaries evaluated several scenarios involving hypothetical risks with loss probability either known or ambiguous. One of these scenarios involved a manufacturing company that wanted to determine the price of a warranty to cover the $100 cost of repairing a component of a personal computer. The questionnaire asked each actuary to estimate premiums for both non-ambiguous and ambiguous probabilities, with losses either independent or perfectly correlated, and p=.001, .01 and .10.

The impact of correlated risks appears when examining the median values of the premiums the actuaries estimated they would charge. If the actuaries express more concern about highly correlated risks than independent ones, it should be reflected in increased premiums. Greater concern for underwriters means an expectation of greater losses. One can compute the ratio of prices charged for correlated risks relative to those for independent risks, for either well-specified or ambiguous risks. Should the actuaries perceive no difference between correlated and independent risks, the premiums would be the same and the ratio of prices would be 1. Should the actuaries perceive reason for concern about correlated risks, the ratio would be greater than 1.

The data presented in Table 4.7 below suggest a great deal of concern about correlated risks. The median premiums for the correlated risks always proved higher than the non-correlated ones, except for well-specified risks with few expected losses and a low probability (p= .001). The ratios became dramatically higher when the risks were ambiguous. In fact, when p= .01, the median premiums for correlated risks were more than 5.5 times that of independent risks.

E. Administrative Costs

The insurer must also be able to recover the costs of analyzing, underwriting, selling and distribution, claim-paying, and meeting the regulatory requirements of issuing insurance policies. Insurers usually calculate these costs, collectively referred to as "administrative expenses," as a percentage of premium dollars paid by an insured.

---

[16] Hogarth, Robin and Howard Kunreuther, "Pricing Insurance and Warranties: Ambiguity and Correlated Risks," *The Geneva Papers on Risk and Insurance Theory*, 17, 1992, pp. 35-60.

Table 4.7. Ratio of Premiums Estimated by Actuaries for Correlated Risks.

	Probability Level		
Nature of Probability	.001	.010	.100
Well-specified (p)	.91	1.2	1.3
Ambiguous (Ap)	2.0	5.6	2.0

II. MARKETABILITY CONDITIONS

Even if an insurer determines that a particular risk meets insurability conditions, the insurer will not invest the time and money to develop a product unless convinced that there is sufficient demand to cover the cost.

Demand for Coverage

There are several factors that normally trigger a business' interest in purchasing insurance. Businesses that have limited assets and/or are risk averse are anxious to transfer the risk of high consequence events to another party rather than bearing it themselves. For example, a company considering the purchase of property may be reluctant to buy if it knows it will have to pay the costs of cleanup should groundwater contamination be discovered on the property in the future.

If the property promises to yield attractive profits, the company may be willing to pay a premium in excess of the actuarially fair cost for having an insurer provide coverage against large future losses. As was discussed earlier, by having this financial protection, firms may be willing to engage in certain activities that they would otherwise avoid if they knew they were subject to a potentially catastrophic loss.

Demand for insurance also stems from third party considerations. Firms seeking capital to invest in certain activities, such as the purchase of property, must demonstrate the security of their financial position to potential lenders. In general, lenders are wary of uninsured losses. For example, banks and financial institutions normally require proof of fire insurance as a condition for issuing a mortgage. They wish to ensure that the owners can pay off the loan if a fire occurs. Similarly, banks and financial institutions sometimes require proof of insurance to cover future environmental cleanup as a condition for issuing a mortgage. They wish to ensure that the owners can pay off the loan under these conditions as well.

The demand for insurance by firms or individuals can also arise from financial responsibility requirements (FRRs). Today, motor vehicle bureaus in many states require individuals to show proof of automobile insurance as a condition for registering their cars or trucks. The Federal Insurance Administration (FIA) requires flood coverage for those residing in specially-designated flood areas who are applying for a federally-insured mortgage. The U.S. EPA imposes FRRs on firms storing waste in underground storage tanks to ensure that they have sufficient funds to compensate victims for environmental damage and/or to restore the surrounding area to its former condition in the event of a tank leak.

There is an additional reason for an owner of a UST to purchase insurance to cover the costs of a leak and the replacement of the tank. Such coverage is likely to serve as a signal to potential customers and other interested parties that the tank is safe. If an insurance company puts its capital on the line by agreeing to cover potential losses from UST leaks, others could interpret insurance as a seal of approval for the tank.[17]

An Illustrative Example

A hypothetical example illustrates how insurance can meet the demands of a commercial enterprise. Alpha Company, a relatively small firm with assets of $100 million, is considering developing and marketing safer underground storage tanks— ones with a much lower probability of leaking than current models. Designing this new tank will require an up-front investment of approximately $1 million. Alpha is so confident that its new tanks will not leak that it is willing to market tanks with the guarantee that, should leakage occur within five years, Alpha will cover the buyer's cost of groundwater cleanup. Alpha's management knows that there is still a chance that one or more of its new tanks will leak during the next five years.

Because Alpha is a closely-held corporation, the owners have a large percentage of their wealth tied up in the firm. They know that any large cleanup expenditures could result in the bankruptcy of the firm. Thus, they are anxious to transfer this risk to an insurance company and are willing to pay a premium somewhat in excess of the actuarially fair value of expected future cleanup costs.

In order to obtain the capital to develop and market this new tank, Alpha must provide a guarantee to its lender that the firm will be able to cover cleanup costs in the event of a leak. One way to meet this third party concern is through the purchase of an insurance policy to cover any groundwater contamination caused by Alpha's tanks.

The potential customers interested in purchasing these tanks also are concerned with the ability of Alpha to pay for the costs of cleanup should a tank leak. Unless these customers remain confident that Alpha is financially sound, they are unlikely to trust the guarantee, or to purchase the product. The fact that Alpha has purchased insurance to cover groundwater cleanup costs could convince potential purchasers of the tank that the product is of high quality. In other words, insurance serves as a seal of approval.

---

[17] Of course, the purchase of insurance by itself does not say anything about the magnitude of the risk. If the tank were risky, the insurer would charge a high premium that the insured could still choose to purchase. The concept of "seal of approval" used here is based solely on the availability of insurance, not the price of coverage.

If Alpha can purchase insurance coverage to satisfy its needs, and those of other interested parties, then both Alpha and the general public benefit. Alpha engages in a new activity that it would not otherwise undertake—i.e., making new tanks. And, the probability and magnitude of groundwater contamination from leaking storage tanks is reduced when new, safer tanks replace old ones.

Role of the Broker

Before concluding this section on marketability, it is important to understand the role of the insurance broker in marketing policies. As we shall see in Chapter 6, distribution can consume almost half of the total costs required for insurance administration. Insurance companies normally rely on brokers to help market their product to commercial enterprises. Most insurance brokers are comfortable with the vast array of traditional products available to corporate customers. However, for coverage against certain risks, e.g., natural hazards and technological or environmental damage, the core of the product may rely upon extensive engineering information, which is often foreign to the non-specialty insurance broker and to the corporate risk manager.

In addition, if coverage relies upon environmental regulations, brokers must familiarize themselves with a new body of knowledge. Changes in regulations and new interpretations by the courts of both environmental law and insurance coverages present an additional sales barrier that brokers must overcome.

Brokers may also have to present environmental insurance options to an entirely new set of corporate decision-makers. Traditionally, the insurance purchase is the sole purview of the corporate risk manager, who selects the insurance based on the options presented by the broker. In the case of coverages such as environmental insurance, a whole new group of managers becomes involved, any of whom may have more authority and decision-making capability than the risk manager. General counsel; operations managers; and vice presidents of acquisition, finance, marketing, or business development may all have a vote in the final purchase of environmental insurance coverage.

Since these policies are new, and limited awareness of their importance exists within corporate structures, companies often neglect the cost of this protection in their budget. Money must often be diverted from other corporate endeavors for insurance. Even more likely, the decision to buy environmental risk insurance remains postponed until money becomes available and corporate decision-makers become more comfortable with the entire concept. This is especially true with voluntary insurance coverage not connected to a specific corporate event, such as the sale of a property.

It is largely the learning and educating tasks, which specialty brokers must perform in order to achieve sales of the environmental insurance product, that determine the level of commissions specialty brokers demand.

III. PRICING THE INSURANCE PRODUCT

The premium that the insurer charges depends on the size of the market for coverage. The size of the market, in turn, depends on the existence of a measurable baseline standard of behavior accepted by all potentially insured parties. Without this standard, it is difficult for the insurer to develop a market for its coverage.

The insurance company will normally not be the one to impose the standard on the market and have it accepted by the relevant parties. Rather, government regulation (e.g., Occupational Safety and Health Administration (OSHA) and EPA specifications for the number of permissible asbestos fibers in the air), industry standards (product specifications by trade associations), or financial institution requirements (e.g., that radon levels must be below a pre-specified level before issuing a mortgage) can all establish uniform standards.

Theoretical Analysis

In specifying a price for its product, the insurance firm relies on its insurability and marketability analyses. The process involves the following two steps:

Step 1: Estimating the Underwriting Premium

This step uses data from the insurability analysis. To initiate this step, there must be some *quantification of risk* by the insurer. This enables the firm to calculate an underwriting premium. The underwriting premium is defined as the expected loss from a given risk without any consideration of the costs of developing and/or marketing coverage. Denote the underwriting premium by R^*. If there is considerable *uncertainty* associated with the risk, then R^* also will reflect the dollar amount that the insurer feels it will have to charge given its attitude toward ambiguity and its degree of risk aversion.

Step 2: Specifying the Breakeven Curve

Once R^* is determined, the insurer calculates the set of premiums it must charge to cover its administrative costs (F) and to make a large enough profit to justify the time and expense invested in obtaining scientific data. The administrative costs include obtaining a statistical database for estimating the risk, calculating the underwriting cost associated with setting the premium using the statistical database, obtaining the necessary regulatory approval to market a policy, and the marketing and distribution costs using a sales force to promote the product.

Define R^*_i as the breakeven premium as a function of the need quantity of insurance sales (Q^*_i) over the lifetime of the product. Figure 4.8 below depicts the set of breakeven premiums ($R^*_i > R^*$) for different values of Q^*_i that the insurer will have to charge when the underwriting premium is $R^*=\$600$ and the fixed costs of developing and marketing are $F=\$1,000,000$. The set of these points comprise the breakeven curve.

Figure 4.8 Breakeven Premiums (R_i) as a Function of Demand for Coverage (Q_i).

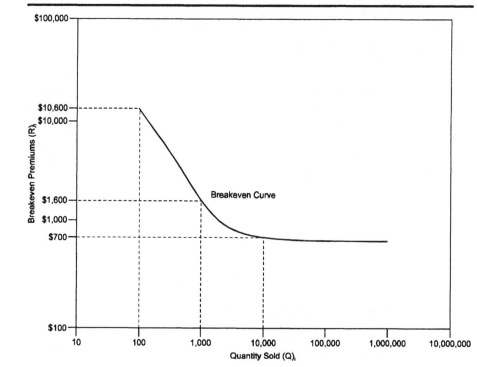

Quantity Sold (Q),

$$R*_i = \$600 + \$1,000,000/Q*_i \qquad (4.2)$$

As $Q*_i$ increases, $R*_i$ decreases because the fixed costs of developing and marketing the insurance are spread over a larger number of policies.

Define Q_i as the actual demand over the lifetime of the product, if the insurer charges a premium $R*_i$. The insurer will only consider marketing coverage if there is at least one $Q_i \ Q*_i$. If there is no premium at which the insurer will at least sell enough policies to break even, the company will elect not to develop and market coverage. If there is more than one point where $Q_i \ Q*_i$, there are two criteria the insurer will use to determine which premium to charge. If the company feels that it has some degree of monopoly power in offering this coverage, it will charge the premium it believes will yield the highest profit. If, on the other hand, it believes that other insurance providers will enter the market as a function of the premium level, it will charge a lower premium to deter other providers from offering the product in order to maintain its monopoly power. This is the curve depicted in Figure 4.8.

From equation (4.2) and Figure 4.8 we see that, if total demand is as low as 1,000, the breakeven premium is $1,600. If demand increases to 10,000 policies, the breakeven premium falls to $700. Should the demand be 100,000 policies, $R*_i$ =

$610, only slightly higher than the underwriting premium.[18] On the basis of an insurer's analysis of the market for UST insurance, for example, the insurer can now estimate whether the demand for coverage at different premiums is likely to exceed the breakeven quantities determined in equation (4.2). If the answer is "yes," UST insurance is developed and marketed. If the answer is "no," the insurer considers the risk uninsurable under the current system.

IV. SUMMARY

This chapter began with an examination of the two broad conditions which must be satisfied for a risk to be **insurable**. The first condition requires the insurer to set a pure premium by quantifying the frequency and magnitude of loss associated with specific events comprising the risk. The second condition specifies a set of factors important to consider, such as adverse selection and moral hazard, when the insurer determines what premium and coverage (e. g., maximum limits, nature of deductible) to offer.

In determining whether there is a **market for insurance,** it is necessary to examine the factors that influence the demand and supply of coverage. Demand normally occurs because the potential policyholder is risk averse and willing to pay a relatively small premium for protection against a large loss. Third parties and financial responsibility requirements also generate demand. Insurers become willing to supply coverage if they can estimate the expected loss from a given risk, and can do so without any consideration of the costs of developing and marketing coverage. They then need to determine whether they can set a premium that will generate enough revenue to cover both the expected loss as well as other costs.

---

[18] Total demand refers to the number of policies sold over a number of years. If a policy is sold in the future it needs to be discounted to the present since the costs of developing and marketing the insurance are assumed to be incurred today. Given a 10 percent discount rate, 1,000 policies sold one year from now would be treated as if only 900 policies were sold.

5

INSURING ASBESTOS RISK: BACKGROUND AND IDENTIFICATION OF RISK

In 1985, pioneers in the environmental insurance industry set out to produce insurance products to fill the gap in coverages left by the exclusion of environmental liability in standard policies. The remainder of this book relies upon the experience of the industry. In the next two chapters, we describe the process involved in creating one of the first of this new generation of environmental insurance products: coverage to address liabilities associated with asbestos in existing facilities. The discussions provide considerable detail regarding the factors considered in creating a new product for this risk. The detail is necessary to link the theory outlined in the last chapter to the actual conditions found in practice. In this chapter, we will begin with a brief overview of the political and economic context surrounding the development of such coverage, and describe the risks associated with asbestos. Chapter 6 utilizes this information to discuss insurability and marketability conditions for the asbestos risk.

I. OVERVIEW OF THE RISK

Asbestos is a naturally-occurring mineral composed of long, silky fibers that have acoustic and insulating qualities. The inhalation of friable[1] asbestos fibers has been linked to three diseases: asbestosis, mesothelioma, and lung cancer. Asbestosis is a chronic disease in which the lungs become scarred as a result of the inhalation of

---

[1] Friable asbestos is easily pulverized and can become airborne.

asbestos fibers. Mesothelioma is a cancer of the lining of the lung or abdominal cavity. Exposure to asbestos fibers increases lung cancer risk. The risk increases geometrically when linked to smoking. Lung cancer is the greatest health-related risk from asbestos exposure.

The health risk to society from asbestos exists because of its widespread use in construction. Due to their acoustic and insulating characteristics, builders used materials containing asbestos widely in North America. From World War II until the ban on asbestos use in new construction in the 1970s, more than 3,000 common construction products used asbestos, including floor tiles, insulation materials, roofing tiles, fireproofing material, and acoustic tile. The U. S. consumed approximately 35 million metric tons of asbestos from 1940 to 1980.[2] Surveys conducted by the U.S. Environmental Protection Agency estimate the presence of asbestos-containing materials in at least 31,000 schools and 733,000 other public and commercial buildings in the U.S. This is approximately 20 percent of all commercial buildings in the nation.[3]

Inevitably, exposure to the tons of asbestos installed in buildings and contained in other products resulted in injuries and deaths. Approximately 24,000 asbestos workers, and others who claimed asbestos exposure and subsequent injury, filed product liability suits against asbestos manufacturers by 1983.[4] These suits cost the industry approximately $1 billion between 1970 and 1982.[5] It was the risk of exposure to this enormous liability that caused traditional insurers to associate asbestos with high risk and high claim costs, and, subsequently, to deny insurance coverage to any party dealing with asbestos.[6]

Regulatory Environment

As a result of the relationship of asbestos to various life-threatening diseases, the federal government, and various state and local governments, have passed legislation or issued regulations concerning the abatement, enclosure, and encapsulation of asbestos. These laws and regulations, promulgated by various agencies, provide well-specified standards for different types of facilities. The regulations include the Clean Air Act (CAA), Toxic Substances Control Act (TSCA), Asbestos School

---

[2] 'Practices and Proceedings for Asbestos Control, 1986, University of Kansas, The National Asbestos Training Center, 1986.

[3] United States Environmental Protection Agency, EPA Study of Asbestos-Containing Materials in Public Buildings: A Report to Congress, February 1988.

[4] Kakalik, James S. et al., Costs of Asbestos Litigation, RAND Institute for Civil Justice, Santa Monica, CA, R-3042–ICJ,1983, p. v.

[5] Ibid.

[6] See Rees, Donald W., 'Have Environmental and Toxic Tort Claims Created an Insurance Crisis: Where Do We Go From Here?' Environmental and Toxic Tort Claims: Insurance Coverage in 1989 and Beyond, Commercial Law and Practice Course Handbook Series Number 495, (A4–4260), Practising Law Institute, New York, 1989, pp. 415–462. This work contains a discussion of insurance availability and, particularly, a report prepared by the United States General Accounting Office entitled "Hazardous Waste: Issues Surrounding Insurance Availability," which was reprinted in Mealey's Litigation Reports: Insurance, 2(1), November 10, 1987.

Hazard Abatement Act (ASHAA), Asbestos Hazard Emergency Response Act (AHERA), Resource Conservation and Recovery Act (RCRA), National Emission Standards for Hazardous Air Pollutants (NESHAP), and Comprehensive Environmental Response, Compensation, and Liability Act (CERCLA).

The Occupational Safety and Health Administration (OSHA) has also promulgated several rules regarding safe asbestos work practices. In July 1989, the EPA issued an Asbestos Ban and Phaseout Rule[7] under TSCA. This rule prohibits the importation, manufacture, and processing of 94 percent of all asbestos products in the United States. The three-part phase-out began in 1990, with completion scheduled by 1997.

In addition to federal regulations, many states and cities, including New York City, have enacted legislation, regulations, or both, to control asbestos. Some states have taken advantage of expanded RCRA authority to classify asbestos-containing wastes as hazardous waste, requiring stringent handling, manifestation (labeling), and disposal procedures.[8] Friable asbestos is also a CERCLA hazardous substance, which may require certain EPA reporting requirements.[9]

Solutions

In dealing with the health risks associated with asbestos, three separate strategies developed. As noted earlier, the first strategy is to severely limit the permitted uses of asbestos in new construction and products. The second is to design a regulatory framework governing permissible procedures for leaving existing asbestos in place. Finally, when asbestos removal occurs, government agencies develop regulations regarding proper procedures for removal and disposal. Chapter 6 analyzes the latter two strategies in greater detail.

II. THE ASBESTOS IN PLACE RISK

Regulations Affecting In Place Asbestos

Maintaining asbestos in place can be a safe and cost-effective method of dealing with asbestos, if handled properly. In an effort to insure a safe process, many of the laws mentioned above have spawned regulations affecting both asbestos in place and asbestos removal. The distinction between the rules that govern asbestos in place and those that apply to asbestos removal have merely been a matter of a few tenths of fiber content per cubic centimeter in sampled air. It is important to realize

---

[7] 40 C. F. R. Section 763 Subpart E.

[8] United States Environmental Protection Agency, *"Managing Asbestos In Place: A Building Owner's Guide to Operations and Maintenance Programs for Asbestos-Containing Materials, Pesticides and Toxic Substances"* (TS-799), 20T-2003, July 1990. p. 28.

[9] Ibid.

that no regulations explicitly *require* asbestos removal, except in larger renovation or demolition projects.

Generally, maintenance of asbestos in place requires the following activities under federal regulation:

1. **Monitoring:** the air in a facility suspected of containing asbestos must be sampled according to certain engineering guidelines to ascertain whether fiber content is at safe levels.

2. **Reporting:** If fiber content is found in the air, a number of notification procedures are mandated. Depending on the situation, the list of notified parties shall include: the EPA, employees and tenants in a building, the parents of students in a school, and/or outside contractors who come into a building to do maintenance, renovation, repairs, or demolition.

3. **Training:** Workers who may come into contact with asbestos during their ordinary duties must be trained to understand the hazards of asbestos and the methods for dealing with a release or disturbance, should one occur. Certain small, short-term projects are not subject to full asbestos removal regulations, but still require worker protection in addition to proper cleanup and disposal procedures. An example of such a project would be drilling into asbestos-containing drywall.

4. **Disposal:** Asbestos must be disposed of using a specified procedure, including proper marking and eventual storage in an approved disposal facility.

A more detailed summary of requirements and procedures appears in Chapter 6 of the EPA's 1990 document entitled *Managing Asbestos In Place: A Building Owner's Guide to Operating and Maintenance Programs for Asbestos-Containing Materials*.[10] The specific regulations cited in that chapter are OSHA Construction Industry Standard for Asbestos,[11] OSHA General Industry Standard for Asbestos,[12] OSHA Respiratory Protection Standard,[13] EPA Worker Protection Rule,[14] EPA National Emission Standards for Hazardous Air Pollutants (NESHAP),[15] and EPA Asbestos Hazard Emergency Response Act (AHERA).[16]

OSHA revised some of its codes[17] regarding asbestos handling. These took effect in October 1995.[18] These rules include a four-tiered classification system describing

---

[10] Ibid.

[11] 29 C. F. R. Section 1926.58.

[12] 29 C. F. R. Section 1910.1001.

[13] 29 C. F. R. Section 1910.134.

[14] 40 C. F. R. Section 763 Subpart G.

[15] 40 C. F. R. Section 61 Subpart M.

[16] 40 C. F. R. Section 763 Subpart E.

[17] 29 C. F. R. Section 1910, 20 C. F. R. Section 1915, and 29 C. F. R. Section 1926.

[18] OSHA's Final Rule for Occupational Exposure to Asbestos was published in 59 Fed. Reg. 153, August 19, 1994.

which work projects correspond to which level of asbestos risk, and further clarify the types of procedures and protection mandated under the new classification system. For asbestos insurability purposes, the changes clearly define harmful dosage levels, adding further specification to the risk characteristics.

Building owners also must survey and sample for asbestos. There are a variety of labeling and notification requirements that accompany the identification of these materials. Many of the additional requirements are similar to those of AHERA and NESHAP regulations, and generally fall into alignment with previous EPA standards.

These changes increase the specificity of work procedures employed by those who might potentially disturb asbestos. In the event that the type of work project done on a facility can be classified as "Class I" or "Class II" under the new four-tiered system, the regulations regarding the removal of asbestos govern the activity.

Risk of Asbestos Remaining in Buildings

The basic risk of asbestos in buildings is a different type of risk from the liabilities that frightened insurers in the 1980s. Rather than a concept with bodily injury resulting from high levels of asbestos exposure or product liability claims, the current risk is that third parties, such as a tenants, will inhale relatively low levels of existing asbestos, become ill, and hold the building owner or manager liable for the injury. This only would occur as a result of either damaged asbestos-containing materials becoming friable, or disturbance of asbestos-containing materials during maintenance, remodeling, demolition, or other activities.

If there is a release of asbestos of the type described, the building owner is subject to a wide range of financial liabilities to third parties, all related to the risk of inhalation. Significant third-party liabilities include: bodily injury arising from exposure to asbestos, property damage (contamination) resulting from an asbestos release, and/or business interruption (removal project) expenses resulting from asbestos release.

Solution—Asbestos Abatement

The solution to managing these risks is in the proper removal and disposal of asbestos-containing materials. The decision to remove and dispose of asbestos often occurs in connection with the renovation or demolition of existing space. In part, this has to do with regulatory requirements, and, in part, with logistical considerations.

The range of asbestos removal projects varies as widely as do the types of facilities to be renovated or demolished. Schools, office buildings, airports, high rise residential facilities, and industrial facilities have all had asbestos removed from their premises, consisting primarily of sprayed-on asbestos fireproofing or acoustical material, and asbestos pipe-covering material. Estimated asbestos abatement in the U. S. will cost approximately $200 billion.

The asbestos rules under NESHAP[19] govern demolition, removal, and renovation of all asbestos-containing materials. Under NESHAP regulations, workers must remove all asbestos-containing materials from a building before demolition, to prevent an asbestos release into the surrounding environment. Asbestos disturbed by renovation also may be governed by work practice rules under NESHAP. In addition, any asbestos removal above specified volumetric parameters (≥ 160 sq. ft. or ≥ 260 ln. ft.), whether or not it is part of a renovation or maintenance procedure, triggers reporting requirements and emission control under specified work practices like those described under OSHA's rules.

The OSHA Construction Industry Standard[20] for asbestos details work procedures for asbestos removal or encapsulation projects, as well as for repair, maintenance, alteration, or renovation of materials containing asbestos.

As previously stated, applicable regulations often require asbestos removal in the event of demolition or renovation. In order to make the discussion of the regulations concerning asbestos abatement more understandable, the following is a simplified description of a typical step-by-step abatement project:

1. Background air monitoring samples are taken to determine the fiber count in the work area before any work is actually begun.

2. The area from which the asbestos is to be removed is isolated by plastic barriers constructed of 6 millimeter polyethylene. The outside area is isolated through the use of yellow plastic ribbon barriers and warning signs.

3. Access to the isolated work area is restricted to passage through a decontamination facility. Regulations require that the facility consist of a "clean" room (where street clothes are stored), a shower facility, and a "dirty" room (where asbestos-contaminated material is kept).

4. All workers entering the contained work site location are required to wear protective clothing and respirators. The type and level of respiratory protection for the workers is set by government standards.

5. The work site area is placed in a slight vacuum through the use of portable air ventilation machinery. The air is ventilated out of the contained work area through a series of filters, the last of which is a high efficiency particulate filter (HEPA). These filters are designed to remove all airborne fibers. This is done to ensure that, if a break in the isolation barrier occurs, air will flow from the outside into the containment location, minimizing the likelihood of an asbestos fiber release outside the containment area. The maintenance of the pressure differential is measured.

---

[19] 40 C. F. R. Section 61 Subpart M.

[20] 29 C. F. R. Section 1926.58.

6. Prior to being disturbed, all asbestos material is saturated with chemicals to reduce the likelihood of fiber release.

7. Asbestos is generally removed by scraping. The work is relatively unskilled.

8. Vacuums with HEPA filters are used to vacuum and bag the wet asbestos material.

9. The asbestos material is then bagged, barrelled, and disposed of in a certified landfill facility.

10. During the entire abatement process, air within and without the abatement location is constantly monitored.

11. Upon completion of the project, the plastic barriers are removed and disposed of as asbestos-contaminated material.

The Abatement Risk

The risk associated with asbestos abatement is the possibility of third-party asbestos fiber exposure from the disturbance of asbestos fiber during the removal process. Exposure can occur when fibers accidentally escape outside the sealed containment barrier surrounding the asbestos removal area. All workers within the containment area are subject to strict medical surveillance and are provided respirators to eliminate the risk of fiber inhalation. However, third parties outside the area, such as workers present in other areas of a building being renovated, are without respiratory protection. Accidental release outside the containment area causes fiber exposure risk for these third parties.

Facility owners who contract to have asbestos removed from their facilities face possible liability and seek protection in the same way they seek protection from the liabilities associated with all construction jobs on their facilities. Generally, they require some type of indemnification from contractors.

Conclusion

This chapter discussed two risks associated with asbestos. The first risk is potential exposure by third parties to asbestos that remains in a building and is somehow disturbed or released through maintenance or remodeling activity. The second risk occurs when asbestos, disturbed during removal, leaks from the containment area of an abatement site and exposes parties without respiratory protection. In both cases, there is a risk of damage to property that may become contaminated with asbestos due to a release.

The risk associated with asbestos is clear. The question, from an insurance perspective, particularly in light of the claims existing from asbestos exposure, remains: "Which asbestos risks are insurable?" The next chapter will address this question using the insurability criteria outlined in Chapter 4.

6

INSURING ASBESTOS RISK: INSURABILITY AND MARKETABILITY CONDITIONS

The last chapter provided an identification of asbestos risks, and an overview of the regulatory history. In this chapter we will briefly review the risks, and examine in detail the factors required to create the insurance product now successfully marketed.

I. INSURABILITY CONDITIONS

As indicated in Chapter 4, the process of assessing insurability involves two conditions: 1) identifying the risk, and 2) setting premiums for specific risks. If the risk is insurable based upon these two conditions, the next question has to do with marketability. Can the premium for the risk be set at a level that stimulates sufficient demand for the product so that a profitable market exists for the insurance?

Condition 1: Identifying the Risk

As seen in Chapter 4, an underwriter's pricing depends to a large degree on whether the probability of an adverse event and the magnitude of a potential loss are well specified. To the degree to which an underwriter can study and understand the probability and magnitude of a risk, the risk premium can more accurately reflect the actual risk involved in the given situation.

Chapter 5 identified and extensively reviewed the core risks associated with asbestos. Those risks might be rephrased as the following questions: "How likely is it that someone will inhale asbestos fibers from an accidental release at a facility and consequently develop an illness?" "In the unfortunate event that someone does develop an illness from asbestos inhalation, how much will it cost to compensate them?"

In attempting to answer these questions, the first step is to analyze their component issues. Answering the question of exposure involves using available knowledge about federal regulations and scientific measurement of asbestos release. Studies on the effects of asbestos on human health reveal information on illness. Creating an estimation of the cost of compensation includes examining the record of existing court cases, and the average payments for asbestos claims in the history of such cases.

Condition 2: Setting Risk Premiums

Risk premium describes the "breakeven" sum an insurer must collect in order to maintain the funds necessary to pay all claims for a given class of risk. Arriving at this amount is essential to determining insurability.

After obtaining and studying the data regarding each risk component, insurers apply them to statistical models. As we show below, there are very similar issues involved in both asbestos removal and asbestos remaining in buildings. Therefore, the statistical exposure and cost models developed for asbestos removal should provide a great deal of the calculations necessary for determining risk for asbestos in place as well.

The following four interrelated factors require examination to arrive at the risk premium: risk ambiguity, adverse selection, moral hazard, and correlative risk.

II. RISK AMBIGUITY FOR ASBESTOS REMOVAL

As described in the asbestos abatement section in the previous chapter, well-defined regulatory standards exist for asbestos removal. EPA and OSHA standards are highly specific for abatement procedures in order to minimize the likelihood of asbestos release outside the area being remediated, remodeled, or demolished. The high level of specificity required by government-mandated compliance provides an excellent means of measuring the asbestos release during removal, assuming compliance by contractors with the regulatory standard.

An examination of air monitoring of asbestos abatement projects established fiber release levels. For contractors who followed government regulations, fiber counts of asbestos during abatement procedures were well below Permissible Exposure Levels (PEL). Regulators recently upgraded the U. S. standard on asbestos fiber exposure to 0.1 fibers per cubic centimeter (f/cc) on an eight-hour Time Weighted Average (TWA) test (stricter than the previous 0.2 f/cc). On average for abatement jobs studied,[1] fiber counts within the containment barrier were .096 f/cc, and outside the containment barrier were .006 f/cc. Consequently, the likelihood of a fiber escape above the exposure level is minimal when contractors employ required work practices.

The data provide the first basis for specifying the probability of an adverse event, which reduces the risk ambiguity for insurers.

The next relevant ambiguity in asbestos risk is the likely number of persons affected by a release if one should occur. Factors to examine when attempting to project this number include building type, occupancy status, and square footage of the abatement project work area. The computation of premium rates may rely on both total contract revenues and asbestos-related revenues as exposure bases.

It is important to take a sample of diverse building types, and to assume densely occupied office space, for the purposes of such a calculation in order to conservatively estimate the exposure level. General estimates for the number of square feet per person range from a low of approximately 120 to 150 square feet for government space, to a high of 300 to 350 square feet for executive suites, such as attorney's offices. The Government Services Administration has published guidelines that government offices should not exceed 135 square feet per person in order to meet standards for cost-effectiveness.

Estimates of the potential number of individuals exposed to an asbestos fiber release use this data. For example, assuming an office building of 30,000 square feet, with an average density of 200 square feet per person, 150 persons probably occupy the building. This is the second method of risk ambiguity reduction.

Risk premium adjustments based on these results can be related to asbestos revenue, yielding figures expressed in terms of the number of persons potentially exposed per thousand dollars of asbestos revenue.

To add further specificity to the probability of illnesses resulting from asbestos inhalation, studies are available describing the health effects of asbestos on humans. Estimates of the health impacts of asbestos exposure rely upon dosage models. Dosage is a function of fiber level exposure measured over time. Summarizing OSHA models, extrapolated to the lower dosages associated with asbestos abatement projects[2], risk models anticipate the increased mortality/morbidity (deaths and injuries) per 10 million persons potentially exposed to asbestos.

For example, suppose we are able to determine that the number of persons exposed per thousand dollars of contract revenue is 10 and the fiber concentration is 0.2 f/cc. By consulting the table of modified OSHA data, we find that the mortality/morbidity probability is 60 out of 10 million persons. Multiplying 60/10 million by 0.2 f/cc results in a 0.000012 claim number per thousand dollars of contract

---

[1] From an unpublished report created by the ERIC Group, Inc., *Property Transfer Insurance: Loss Model for Statute Driven Liability,* March 29, 1991.
[2] Obenchain, Thomas, *Risk Report of Asbestos Induced Mortality/Morbidity,* 1988. Unpublished report.

revenue. Using the mortality/morbidity figures in this way represents the third method of reducing the ambiguity in asbestos-related injury probabilities.

The last method is specifying the magnitude of potential loss. This component of ambiguity reduction seeks to establish the average payment amount likely for each health claim filed. Chapter 2 examined studies prepared by the RAND Institute for Civil Justice in some detail. These studies revealed that the average total compensation paid plaintiffs in asbestos liability cases was $60,000. This figure provides a basis from which to estimate upwards the likely loss associated with the asbestos liability in commercial buildings.

For example, suppose the $60,000 (1982 dollars) doubled to $120,000 (in present dollars). Multiplying the average claim amount by the expected number of claims per thousand dollars of contract revenue (shown in the previous section) yields $120,000 X 0.000012 = $1.44 ultimate cost per thousand dollars of contract revenue.

The claim costs figures add further precision to the risk premium calculation by specifying the likely magnitude of an asbestos liability loss and determining what the ultimate costs might be.

In order to determine the risk premium for asbestos removal, it is necessary to identify ambiguity about the risks of injury resulting from an asbestos removal. In the case of asbestos removal, the estimate of probability of the adverse event was specified by examining probable fiber exposure level, probable number of parties exposed in the event of a release, and information about disease manifestation at various exposure levels. The probable magnitude of a loss is estimated using the history of awards in court cases involving asbestos liability. The examination of this information removes a great degree of the ambiguity from the risk premium determination and helps the risk premium reflect the actual risk.

III. RISK AMBIGUITY FOR ASBESTOS IN PLACE

Dealing with the unknowns for asbestos remaining in buildings follows a process very similar to that of asbestos removal. The adverse event is the same: Third-party inhalation of asbestos fibers and subsequent injury due to accidental release.

As with asbestos removal, well-defined regulatory standards exist for asbestos left in buildings. Specifying potential exposure requires an understanding of the regulations and information about the likelihood of release given compliance with standards. The differences between the regulations regarding asbestos in buildings and asbestos removed primarily deal with monitoring the condition of the asbestos. If asbestos remains undisturbed and non-friable, the chances of fiber release remain small. The standards require little beyond identification and notification of the location of the asbestos-containing material. If asbestos is disturbed, a continuum from minor repair work to full-blown asbestos removal requirements is triggered, based upon the 1995 OSHA classification system.

As discussed earlier, the health risk attributable to asbestos fibers is dosage related. Dosage is a function of both the level of exposure and the length of time of the exposure. For facilities containing asbestos materials, there are very low levels of exposure (often zero) over long periods of time. This contrasts with the asbestos removal model, which has higher levels of exposure over shorter durations. Both examples use the OSHA model relating dosage to health risk.

The number of exposed persons at risk for asbestos in place is different than the number at risk during asbestos removal. An accidental release potentially exposes all occupants and visitors to a building. The data and actuarial equations used in determining probability figures for asbestos removal can be mathematically extrapolated to determine probability in this situation.

Essentially, the example used in the prior section on asbestos removal applies here as well. The difference lies in that, instead of calculating the number of persons exposed per thousand dollars of contract revenue, the numbers are converted to persons potentially exposed per square foot.

Differences between types of facilities are taken into account. In apartment buildings where people spend a great deal of time, risk is somewhat higher. In shopping centers, the risk is somewhat lower, since most visitors stay in those facilities only for a short period of time.

As mentioned above, asbestos exposure relies upon dosage, and dosage is a function of fiber level exposure measured over time. In the removal process, the risk is generally higher in the short term, since there are typically a greater number of fibers present over a shorter period of time. In the asbestos-in-place situation, a better description of the dosage is as low levels of exposure over longer periods of time. The mortality/morbidity models created to evaluate risk associated with the removal process also have application to the asbestos in place model, once the differences in the dosage model are taken into account.

The costs of asbestos claims for the removal process also apply to the asbestos in place model.

The data used to determine risk premium for asbestos removal also apply to the determination of risk premium for asbestos-in-place.

Calculations assessing the potential asbestos exposure to persons relied upon specifying the differences in dosage created by the asbestos in place situation. Where asbestos removal can cause relatively high dosage exposure in a short amount of time, asbestos in place is more likely to create low dosage exposure over a longer period of time. A risk premium determination depends upon an understanding of this model.

Asbestos Removal and Asbestos in Place: Comprehensive Summary and Conclusion

In order to determine the amount of premium required to cover potential losses due to accidental asbestos release, a full understanding of the risks is necessary. Determining risk premium for asbestos removal and asbestos remaining in buildings followed a similar pattern of analysis, occurring in a four-stage review of scientific data. The four parameters of ambiguity studied for asbestos risks were: potential levels of exposure in case of accidental asbestos release, the potential number of persons exposed to accidentally released asbestos, the likelihood of contracting an illness after asbestos exposure, and the cost of compensating a person who has become ill due to asbestos exposure.

Studying available scientific data transforms what was an unspecified risk into a well-specified risk by defining the risk parameters. While underwriters generally assess risk based on historical fact, basing assumptions about asbestos risk on scientific study allows the development of a risk premium that relies on scientific fact when there are no historical data available.

Given this examination of the means to resolve risk ambiguity and determine risk premium, the discussion continues with an examination of additional risk phenomena that can affect risk premium.

IV. ADDITIONAL INSURABILITY BARRIERS

Adverse Selection

As pointed out in Chapter 4, an additional concern in setting risk premiums is adverse selection. With respect to asbestos, the key underwriting issues for adverse selection relate to compliance with government standards. Underwriters may consider property owners and contractors who comply with government regulations good risks and ones who do not, bad risks. Sorting the good from the bad often includes a review of internal operating procedures of the potential insureds, monitoring performance, and inspecting their operations to ensure compliance. Furthermore, compliance with government regulations is a prerequisite for contractor licensing.

Moral Hazard

Moral hazard poses no special risk in asbestos coverage. Once adverse selection is overcome through the selection of "non-careless" building owners or abatement contractors, there should be little concern about careless behavior by the insured party since insurance coverage is in place. There seems to be no advantage for a building owner or abatement contractor to purposefully expose his or her property/project to airborne, friable asbestos, since there is no direct benefit. Standard procedures for dealing with moral hazard outlined in Chapter 4, such as the use of deductibles and self-insured retentions, will be sufficient to prevent it.

Correlated Risk

The only potential for correlated risks is the possibility that standards of liability may change. If the liability of the insured increases, and the likelihood of a claim increases, risk premium calculations could become invalid. A study of the regulatory environment should include a check of the likelihood of change in standards of liability. In the case of asbestos liability, standards are unlikely to change. The analysis of asbestos-related issues has been in progress for ten years, and the dust of debate has settled; regulations are firmly in place.

In addition, target markets for asbestos insurance exist in locations and are of various types.

Conclusion

There are no significant barriers to insurability of the risks associated with asbestos in existing facilities. Pricing hinges on assessment of the ambiguities, calculated stringently through the acquisition of scientific underwriting data on the potential insured. The underwriting data takes the form of four levels of analysis: potential fiber exposure, potential exposure of persons to fiber, potential illness resulting from fiber exposure, and costs of compensation. The specification of these parameters hinges primarily on compliance with federal regulations surrounding the handling of asbestos. Once the underwriter receives assurances about the insured's compliance with federally-mandated regulations, the risk becomes predictable. Studying claim payments in court cases specifies the magnitude of the risk.

Adverse selection, moral hazard, and correlated risk phenomena do not generally affect the insurability of asbestos risks. The gathering of underwriting data negates adverse selection effects, and the other barriers to insurability are not likely to significantly impact loss experience. The analysis of the above factors developed a risk premium based on scientific data. Since this data allowed the calculation of the "breakeven" premium (see Figure 4.8, page 52), further estimation of insurability involves a determination of the costs and feasibility of administering and marketing a potential product.

V. ADMINISTRATIVE COSTS

While determining the risk premium is a giant step towards assessing the viability of an insurance product, it, alone, remains insufficient to bring an insurance product to market. The professional insurance provider must be able to recover not only the risk premium, but also the costs of analyzing, underwriting, selling, claim-paying, and meeting the regulatory requirements of issuing insurance policies. Generally speaking, these costs, collectively referred to as administrative expenses, are calculated as a percentage of premium dollars paid by an insured.

The following represents a breakdown of administrative costs by percentage of premium dollars:

Administrative	10%
Commissions	15%
Taxes & Fees	5%
Total:	30%[3]

The following is a brief description of each cost component.

Administrative

This category encompasses four primary costs: underwriting, customer service, regulatory compliance, and general and administration. Underwriting costs reflect screening and monitoring potential insureds. Underwriters trained in the engineering procedures and technical details of the risk work to assess the appropriate pricing based upon risk characteristics given in the potential insured's application.

In addition to underwriting costs, insurance is a highly regulated industry. The costs of complying with state regulations regarding forms, rates, and coverages often can be expensive and time consuming. It is not unusual for the application and filing process for a state license to take upwards of a full year. Annual compliance with state regulations is a significant ongoing expense.

The customer service and general and administrative costs of an insurance company are similar to those of other service-based industries.

Commissions

This category describes the fees paid to brokers and agents for the distribution of insurance products. Brokers generally have access to several insurance companies and seek competing quotations from them in order to obtain (1) the best coverage and price for the customer, and (2) the highest commission for themselves.

The activities and motivations of the brokers have a significant effect on the insurance market. In particular, the willingness of brokers to provide assistance for products requiring specialized expertise is often a function of the commission rate available. Generally, 15 percent is an average figure for brokers supporting specialized lines, including environmental coverages. Currently, there is a downward trend in distribution fees, as noted in Chapter 3.

---

[3] From an unpublished report created by the ERIC Group, Inc., prepared by Alan Potter. However, similar figures also appear in: *Best's Aggregates and Averages - Property-Casualty: 1993 Edition,* A. M. Best, Oldwick, NJ, 1993, p. 157.

Taxes & Fees

The five percent figure shown above is an average estimation of taxes and fees on insurance. Each state has its own set of regulations and fee structures associated with insurance, in addition to regulatory compliance fees.

Conclusion

The premium charged for insurance coverage must, at a minimum, absorb the risk premium and the administrative costs associated with the insurance coverage sold. Further, insurance companies must perceive that there is the opportunity for profit. With respect to those risks whose pricing relies more upon interpretation of scientific data than on historical, actuarial models, the profit opportunity must be significant to compensate for the risk associated with the modeling technique chosen.

The next step is to determine whether a market exists for the insurance product at a price to cover the risk premium and administrative expenses, and to provide a reasonable profit. The task is to determine if the product will sell at the required pricing strategies.

VII. MARKETABILITY OF THE PRODUCT

Even if a risk is quantifiable and an insurance policy created, there is no assurance that anyone will be willing to purchase coverage. Without a market for insurance, a risk is still uninsurable.

Therefore, the final task is to evaluate the conditions necessary for insurance to sell. Most often, insurance is not purchased solely to transfer risk. There are other factors at work that influence an insurance purchase decision.[4] In the asbestos area, insurance purchases often meet third-party requirements. For example, the standard forms of the American Institute of Architects for contract work contain the requirement that contractors purchase insurance against their liabilities prior to the commencement of work.[5]

Building owners who have work performed by contractors generally require some type of indemnification against liabilities associated with the work. For many contractors, the solution to this requirement has been to purchase commercial general liability policies. Building owners generally request proof of insurance from contractors to assure themselves that a financially viable company will be responsible for liabilities arising from the contractor's work. Sophisticated building owners even require that the insurance carrier be highly rated by one of the top rating agen-

---

[4] Hall, Evelyn, "EIL is Poised for Growth," *Best's Review - Property-Casualty Insurance Edition*, A.M. Best, 95(12), April 1995, pp. 40–44.

[5] "General Conditions of the Contract for Construction." *AIA Document A201. 1987 Edition*. American Institute of Architects, Washington, D.C.,1987. Article 11, Sections 11.1–11.3, pp. 19–21.

cies to assure themselves that the financial institution assuming the risk from the construction contractor is sound.

Once insurance became available for contractors performing asbestos removal work, the construction industry created instant demand for the coverage.[6] In fact, such insurance became a virtual license to do business. Between 1987 and 1992, the annual premiums paid for specialty asbestos coverage grew to $100 million, 20% of the $500 million environmental insurance business.[7]

In the case of asbestos remaining in facilities, the purchase of liability insurance is a function of the risk aversion of the facility owner. The market demand among building owners for the purchase of insurance for *asbestos in place* risks has not been as strong as the demand among contractors for *asbestos removal* coverages. This is due to the fact that there is no third-party requirement for building owners to maintain insurance for asbestos in place. This voluntary feature has made it difficult to penetrate the market. The pricing tends to be closer to the risk premium in order to stimulate demand. The total annual premium for purchases of this coverage is approximately $2 million per year.[8]

If building owners have large capital reserves within their own firm, they are less likely to purchase insurance. Firms with annual revenues of $100 million or less spent four times as much of their annual revenue (expressed as a percentage) on insurance premiums for liability coverages than firms with $5 billion or more in revenue, and retained 20% less risk.[9] Consequently, the larger the firm, the less likely it is to purchase coverage as measured by insurance purchase as a percentage of revenue.[10]

VIII. CHAPTER CONCLUSION

Demand for asbestos liability insurance by contractors is high for asbestos removal, generating premiums of $100 million annually. One primary reason for this success is financial responsibility requirements. Most firms purchasing coverage have less than $100 million in annual revenue.[11] The demand for asbestos-in-place insurance for property owners is more limited. The mere transfer of the liability is generally insufficient motivation for owners to purchase insurance. Clearly, the risks associated with asbestos have proved to be marketable.

---

[6] Vogel, Todd, "Critical Industries: There's Gold in Asbestos for This Year's No. 1," *Business Week*, May 23, 1988, p. 122.

[7] Quint, Michael, "Insuring Environmental Liabilities," *The New York Times*, February 17, 1994.

[8] Based on sales reports.

[9] *1994 Cost of Risk Survey*, Towers Perrin Risk Management Publications, Stamford, CT, and Risk and Insurance Management Society, Inc., New York, 1995, Table 5, p. 39.

[10] See also the publication *Engineering News Record* for their annual report of asbestos contractors and annual revenues.

[11] Ibid.

IX. COMPREHENSIVE SUMMARY OF CHAPTERS 5 AND 6

Building upon the analysis in Chapter 4, Chapter 5 provided an overview of risks surrounding asbestos. Beginning with a description and analysis of historical asbestos risks, findings included the recognition that current asbestos risks primarily involve health impacts on persons working in facilities where asbestos remains. These health impacts result from the inhalation of asbestos fibers. Causes include asbestos in existing facilities becoming friable or being disturbed as part of the asbestos removal process.

Chapter 6 reviewed the insurability and marketability conditions of asbestos risk. Federal regulations dealing with asbestos are well specified. Using the federal regulations as a standard of behavior, it was possible to develop data on likely fiber exposure levels from existing asbestos material. Submitting available data to statistical analysis permitted reasonable predictions regarding the probability and magnitude of losses from asbestos exposure. The analysis permitted the calculation of risk premium. There is minimal impact on the risk premium from adverse selection, moral hazard, and correlated risks with respect to asbestos-related risks. The risk premium, combined with administrative expenses, is the minimum premium an insurer must collect to issue a new coverage.

This assessment completed, it remained only to determine whether a market existed for the insurance at a price above the minimum premium. Since building owners require indemnification from contractors in order for them to perform work, a strong motivation existed for contractors to purchase asbestos insurance as a condition of performing asbestos removal work. A less significant demand for asbestos coverage exists for building owners concerned about the risks of asbestos left in their facilities.

Insurance coverage is available to assume the risks associated with asbestos remaining in commercial facilities. The risk is insurable and the product marketable.

7

INSURING OTHER TYPES OF
ENVIRONMENTAL RISK

The last two chapters detailed the determination of a risk, namely asbestos in existing facilities, as insurable and marketable. The discussion described the performance of the resulting new insurance coverages. In this chapter, we examine insurability issues related to three other types of environmental risk, also tested in the market: (1) Property owner liability for environmentally contaminated property, (2) underground storage tanks, and (3) lead-based paint abatement. Only coverage for property owner liability is being successfully marketed. The other two risks encountered significant insurability and marketability issues during product development efforts.

Rather than detailing with each element of the insurability equation for each product, this chapter focuses on the specific components of the risk that affect insurability. In the case of liability for environmental contamination on a property, the significant issue for developing insurance was its marketability. For the underground storage tank (UST) problem, the creation of highly-subsidized State Guarantee Funds has made it difficult for private insurers to market coverage. Vague regulatory standards do not provide an effective means of dealing with the risks associated with lead-based paint abatement. Thus, this potential coverage fails the well-specified and accepted performance standards condition essential to limit the risk's ambiguity.

I. LIABILITY FOR ENVIRONMENTALLY CONTAMINATED PROPERTY

Regulatory Environment

As described in Chapter 2, the Comprehensive Environmental Response, Compensation, and Liability Act, commonly known as CERCLA or Superfund, was enacted to address problems resulting from releases of hazardous substances into the environment from properties previously contaminated with hazardous materials. Generally, these properties no longer actively handle hazardous materials.

CERCLA authorized the imposition of strict liability for the cost of remediating contaminated property upon a broad class of potentially responsible parties (PRPs). Court decisions have construed CERCLA in a way that imposes liability on a very broad basis, with the goal of putting substantial pressure on those responsible for creating the contamination to clean it up. This liability extends to a new purchaser of property. The new owner assumes liability for past activity related to the property, regardless of whether the owner contributed to the contamination.[1] In limited circumstances, a lender to a new owner may also become enmeshed in the liability web.[2] As one can imagine, this potential liability can have a significant, chilling impact on property acquisition.

Most states have enacted statutes that impose liability similar to CERCLA at a state level. In all, there are 112 state Superfund and underground storage tank statutes that impose liability related to hazardous materials on owners of real property.

In order to protect themselves financially, purchasers and lenders often rely on the results of a Phase I preacquisition site assessment to identify any potential preexisting contamination.[3] Standard preacquisition site assessments, limited in scope, consist of five principal components:

1. Examination of the chain of title.

2. Review of aerial photography.

3. Determination of the existence of environmental liens against the property.

4. Review of federal, state, and local government records relating to the use or release of hazardous substances on the property.

5. A visual site inspection.

---

[1] Freeman, Paul K., "The Risk Manager and Property Transfer Environmental Ghosts," *Risk Management*, Risk and Insurance Management Society, February 1992.

[2] Zolkos, Rodd, "Lending Banks a Hand on Superfund," *Business Insurance*, Crain Communications, Chicago, October 2, 1995, pp. 17–20; and Hector, Gary, "A New Reason You Can't Get A Loan," *Fortune*, September 21, 1992.

[3] Sibley, Glen E., "Environmental Insurance," *Urban Land*, ULI-The Urban Land Institute, Washington, D.C., July 1992.

Generally, there is no testing or sampling in a Phase I preacquisition site assessment.[4]

Overview of the Risks

The risk to property owners is that they will incur the rather substantial present liability for environmental remediation as a result of past contamination on their property. The risk becomes somewhat mitigated by engaging in site assessments to attempt to uncover any prior contaminating activity before purchasing property.

Though seldom held liable, even highly-skilled environmental engineers sometimes miss contamination when performing a site assessment. Environmental engineering consultants routinely attach a liability disclaimer to their assessment and, even when there is no disclaimer, the average environmental consultant's errors & omissions insurance is insufficient to protect a property owner who contracts for their services. Therefore, if a property owner or lender has a standard Phase I site assessment performed, and the assessment fails to detect the contamination before property purchase, the owner and lender face exposure to potentially huge environmental liability. Without any method to more effectively mitigate against these environmental risks, corporations and property owners can experience significant delays in transferring property and may be vulnerable to major losses. To deal with this problem, insurers have attempted to develop an insurance policy to transfer the risk of the potential environmental cleanup liability associated with acquiring real property.

Insurability Conditions

The insurability of the risk of environmental cleanup expense is dependent on several interrelated factors. The critical component is a clear analysis of the conditions upon which liability actually becomes imposed on purchasers of real properties. This analysis entails a review of nearly 200 federal and state statutes that are descendants of, or related to, CERCLA. Further understanding requires an analysis of the conditions upon which theoretical liabilities actually become imposed. Further segmentation of the analysis helps to understand the nature of the claims for liability, i.e., remediation of property, offsite claims for contamination, etc.

Condition 1: Identifying the Risk

With the legal framework in hand, it is important to understand how many properties may be subject to liability for pre-existing conditions through a review of engineering data. In addition, if liability is imposed, an estimation of its magnitude requires a determination of the magnitude of potential claims in related court cases.

---

[4] American Society for Testing and Measurement, "E 1527–94," Standard Practice for Environmental Site Assessments: Phase I Environmental Site Assessment Process, ASTM, Philadelphia, PA, 1994.

Studying these insurability issues requires the existence of engineering information sources and records of court cases to quantify the severity and frequency of claims. Since the key to assuming the risk is to limit acceptance to only those properties where no known, easily-detected contamination is present, an understanding of contaminated property identification is essential. Gathering information through an engineering study, which involves inspection of potentially-insured locations, is essential to limit both the adverse selection and the moral hazard associated with the risk. Insurability requirements therefore necessitate establishing minimum environmental review standards for auditing property conditions.

The contamination rate for commercial properties has averaged about 12 percent nationally. A study of 9,000 environmental audits provided this figure.[5] This rate is the percentage of properties with contamination in excess of permissible government exposure levels. Of contaminated properties, estimates indicate that pre-acquisition site assessments will, within statistically defined limits, fail to detect contamination 40 percent of the time.[6] This figure is incorporated into actuarial modeling regarding the likelihood of contamination.

To estimate the potential losses associated with contamination not detected by a pre-acquisition assessment, an examination of the costs of federal and state mandated cleanups at more than 3,000 sites was conducted. Available data indicates that the average cost of remedial action (CORA) ranges from $102,000 for underground storage tanks (USTs) to just over $33 million for Federal National Priority List (NPL) sites (1991 dollars).[7]

Once potential loss frequency (failure to discover contamination) and ranges of severity are understood, the issue becomes one of determining geographic and demographic distribution. A legal model based on 200 federal and state statutes was constructed for this purpose, providing an added degree of specificity to the estimated likelihood of a loss.

Condition 2: Setting the Risk Premium

On the basis of the above data, it is possible to determine the risk premium using the methods discussed in Chapters 4, 5 and 6. The gross figure for the number of contaminated properties can be determined, the average cost of cleanup discovered, and the likelihood of contamination being detected on a property calculated. A figure for the amount of loss allocation could then be calculated, yielding the risk premium.

[5] See an article regarding the study in: "Site Assessment: Insurance Sets Standards," *Engineering News Record*, Mc-Graw Hill, June 17, 1991; and Feder, Barnaby J., "Making a Difference: New Policy on Pollution," *The New York Times*, June 9, 1991.
[6] "Site Assessment: Insurance sets standards," *Engineering News Record*, Mc-Graw Hill, June 17, 1991; and Freeman, Paul K., "The Risk Manager and Property Transfer Environmental Ghosts," *Risk Management*, Risk and Insurance Management Society, February 1992.
[7] University of Tennessee Hazardous Waste Remediation Project. Waste Management Research and Education Institute, *State and Private Sector Cleanups*, University of Tennessee, Knoxville, TN, December 1991. p. 19.

As discussed in Chapter 4, additional risk phenomena include adverse selection, moral hazard, and correlative risk. The potential for either adverse selection or moral hazard in property transfer coverage could be the result of the insurer being unaware of easily detectable risks. Adverse selection would occur if an easily detectable risk passed insurer scrutiny, without minimum environmental review. Moral hazard might occur when the property owner already knows of a risk, and purchases insurance to cover a planned detection. Neither one of these phenomena is possible, however, as long as minimum environmental review is performed prior to the acceptance of any risk.

Nor is correlative risk a significant factor if cleanup standards do not change significantly. The only potential for multiple losses from a single event would come from contamination migrating from one property to several covered properties. Minimum environmental review should eliminate risks where this is a possibility.

Conclusion

Existing property transfer liability insurance has been designed for commercial properties, as opposed to industrial or residential properties. Study of the regulatory environment leads to increased certainty about liabilities. Study of engineering data and court cases results in improved certainty with regard to loss probability and magnitude. The institution of minimum environmental review as a condition of insurance prevents risk phenomenon such as adverse selection and correlative risk. Once a risk premium determination is completed, coverage is technically possible. However, the test of marketability remains.

Marketability Issues

Since property transfer liability insurance is not expressly required by regulation, it cannot be marketable until the potential customers —property owners, buyers, and lenders— are independently motivated to buy a policy. In fact, the insurance solution requires that these customers make two purchase decisions: (1) to purchase the preacquisition site assessment, and (2) to purchase insurance dependent on the results of the site assessment.

The experience with existing products showed that, initially, potential customers were only willing to purchase site assessments. Until these customers became accustomed to purchasing the site assessments and understood their inherent limitations, they were unwilling also to purchase insurance. It thus became necessary to understand the conditions upon which individuals involved in commercial real estate transactions were willing to make the combined site assessment and insurance purchase decision.

Focus groups

Understanding the willingness of this market to pay for the property transfer liability insurance products now sold involved careful study through the use of focus groups. The shift toward market acceptance of environmental assessment of property was vividly demonstrated in videotapes of more than 30 focus groups conducted across the country over a two-year period from 1991 to 1992.[8]

When the focus groups began in 1991, the research subjects were all vice presidents of acquisition from the country's largest development and investment companies. Initially, the subjects reported ordering environmental assessments on properties only with suspected contamination. However, during the eighteen months of the study, subjects reported requiring assessments as standard practice on all properties. The same attitudinal change occurred in the lending industry. Within eighteen months, the majority of the nation's banks began to require assessments as preconditions for most bank-financed real estate transactions.[9]

There were several reasons for this change. First, the American Society for Testing and Measurement (ASTM) designed an agreed-upon site assessment protocol, and the standard achieved wide acceptance in the marketplace. Second, the federal government began to require national banks to conduct environmental due diligence as a component of their lending practices. Today, the assessment process is the cornerstone of the Federal Deposit Insurance Corporation (FDIC) compliance process. In its "Guidelines for an Environmental Risk Program," the FDIC requires that all FDIC-insured banks develop specific risk assessment policies. Finally, nongovernment agencies involved in rating debt instruments based on real estate cash flows have incorporated assessments into their due diligence process.[10] These indirect mechanisms combined to institutionalize an environmental standard that provides a basis for insurance. Using the parameters of the assessment, an insurer can assume the residual liability.

Product Refinement

The remaining marketing issue was whether potential customers would be willing to absorb both the cost of the environmental assessment and the property transfer liability insurance. In part, it was also critical to the sale of property transfer coverage that the cost of the insurance be included in the overall closing costs for the sale of a property. Compared to the overall cost of a commercial property transaction, the cost of the insurance as a budgeted expense becomes nearly insignificant. The ultimate marketing task, therefore, is to establish property transfer liability insur-

---

[8] See Gallagher, Mary Ellen, "Insuring Success: Focus Groups Guide Creation of Environmental Insurance Product," *Quirk's Marketing Research Review*, December 1991.

[9] Subsequent general survey results have confirmed the trends identified in the market research work. See Bennett, Mark J., "Survey Shows Lenders' Widespread Adoption of Environmental Risk Management Policies," *Real Estate/Environmental Liability News*, May 10, 1993, (Part 2).

[10] "Credit Review," *Commercial Mortgage Securities*, Standard & Poor's, March 8, 1993, p. 9.

ance as part of the complete environmental risk management and due diligence package required to close a sale.

Limited Acceptance

Since being introduced as a new product in 1992, property transfer liability coverage has received market acceptance on a limited basis. Sales of the product have been approximately $5–10 million per annum; in excess of $1.5 billion in property has been insured.[11]

The use of this form of environmental insurance has generated significant data on losses from pre-existing contamination on standard commercial property. And a byproduct of the underwriting process is the identification of existing contamination. Underwriting environmental insurance has therefore encouraged the remediation of properties with contamination. Oftentimes, subsequent remediation occurs on a voluntary basis.

The product has not been widely used on all standard property acquisitions. Rather, its use applies to specific instances where a third party (usually the financing institution) requests the insurance as an added layer of protection. In some instances, the insurance may act as a substitute for indemnification or as a specific reserve account for environmental claims. In contrast to the asbestos coverage described in the previous chapter, no compelling industry-driven motivation to purchase this insurance exists.

Summary and Future Directions

CERCLA laws, developed to address problems from hazardous waste release not covered under RCRA, imposed broad liability on property owners for pre-existing contamination. Property owners face the risk of liability for that contamination and subsequent remediation expenses. To protect themselves, owners often have environmental assessments performed on their property. Banks also have increasingly required site assessments as a requirement for loans, particularly since compliance with the FDIC requires due diligence for potential liabilities.

However, approximately 12 percent of commercial properties are contaminated. Approximately 40 percent of site assessments on these properties are inaccurate. The remaining risk this represents is potentially dangerous and costly for property owners and their lenders, and can inhibit property transfer. Insurance can assume this risk. The risk is insurable from both a statistical and scientific perspective. Marketing the insurance requires parties to a property transfer to regard the insurance as part of a package of budgeted environmental risk management, along with site assessment. Because this happened to a limited degree, property transfer liability insurance has received only limited acceptance in the marketplace.

---

[11] Based on sales reports.

However, the benefits of this type of insurance are increasingly recognized by those participating in commercial property portfolio transactions. The insurance covers entire portfolios, thus removing the risk of a potential environmental discovery in a large group of properties.[12] In addition, independent, private credit rating agencies are beginning to recognize the value of insurance as both a due diligence and financial security vehicle.[13]

II. UNDERGROUND STORAGE TANKS

The potential damage to America's groundwater resources from leaking underground storage tanks (USTs) is significant. The Environmental Protection Agency estimates that there are more than 1.4 million USTs used for petroleum storage by fuel distributors, municipalities, and industrial firms and that as many as 35 percent of those tanks could be leaking. As of 1992, there have been 185,000 confirmed releases with the total cost of remediation estimated to be between $30 and $40 billion.[14] Since over one-half of the U. S. population relies on groundwater for drinking,[15] the potential impact from leaking tanks could be the most critical environmental problem in the nation.

Regulatory Environment

The federal government has extensively analyzed the procedure for controlling the risk associated with underground storage tanks. This resulted in comprehensive regulations addressing the operation, maintenance, replacement, and insurance of the tanks. The concept behind the regulations was to make existing owners responsible for costs associated with the leakage of material from their tanks.

Beginning in 1984, Congress and the EPA undertook a comprehensive program initiating the implementation of regulation for USTs. The regulatory scheme, originally adopted from the signing of the Hazardous and Solid Waste Amendments to RCRA, placed USTs under EPA regulatory jurisdiction. EPA's mandate extended in 1988 with the Superfund Amendments and Reauthorization Act (SARA), which had two provisions dealing with USTs. First, Congress demanded that tank owners demonstrate that they could bear financial responsibility in the event of leaks. Sec-

---

[12] Note that correlative risk does not become a problem in portfolio coverage, insofar as properties within the portfolio are diversely located. Environmental insurance underwriters will use location diversity as a criteria of insurability when assessing a portfolio risk. The correlative risk for a portfolio exists when, for example, several independently insured properties (with independent limits of liability) are located above the same aquifer. In this example, a single contamination discovery may trigger several policies at once.

[13] See Standard & Poor's Real Estate Finance, Insurance Requirements, Property Insurance, Environmental Insurance. See also Standard & Poor's, *Credit Review*, Standard & Poor's Corp. Executive and Editorial Offices, New York, March 8, 1993, p. 9.

[14] "USTs: A Busy Decade Ahead," *Environmental Times*, Nov. 1992, p. 31.

[15] Bodgett and Copeland, 1985.

ond, a Leaking Underground Storage Tank Trust Fund was established to clean up leaks untraceable to an owner. The trust fund was financially supported by a 1/10 cent tax on each gallon of gasoline sold.

By 1987, EPA issued UST regulations and standards for testing, modification, replacement, and financial responsibility. The financial responsibility requirements became quite stringent, requiring $1 million per claim and $5 million aggregate coverage. The regulations stipulated that private insurance, as well as other means, might meet the financial responsibility requirements.

During September and October 1988, the EPA published its "final" rules on UST regulation. Businesses would be required to show financial responsibility in stages, depending on the size of the business. The smallest companies were given until October 1990 to comply. The rules were much less stringent than the rules proposed the previous year, a shift attributed to pressure from industry groups.[16]

These "final" rules are currently in force. They require demonstration of financial ability to cover both the cost of any corrective action as well as compensation for third party liability from accidental releases. Per-occurrence coverage is set at either $500,000 or $1 million, depending on the nature of the facility operation and the quantity of the product being handled. Aggregate annual coverage is set at $1 million or $2 million, depending on the number of USTs to be covered.[17]

As with asbestos pollution, regulations provided well-specified guidelines for the operation, maintenance, and replacement of the tanks. Private insurers, well-positioned to take on the role of financial guarantor, thus began to develop coverages.

During 1989, the financial responsibility requirements for the two groups of businesses owning the largest number of USTs went into effect. However, small business and the Congressional committees dealing with small business put pressure on the EPA to postpone requirements for smaller firms. *The New York Times* reported in a front page story that UST regulations were forcing many small gas stations out of business.

At the same time, groups such as the Petroleum Marketers Institute were predicting that 25 percent of the country's service stations would go out of business. In response to political pressure, the EPA allowed the states to develop State Guarantee Funds (SGFs) to satisfy the UST rules. These funds, supported through gasoline sales taxes and/or annual fees, provide tank owners with the required financial protection. Under a typical plan, the fund financing occurs through flat rate taxes on gasoline sales or deliveries, ranging from .1 to 2 cents per gallon, and/or annual operator fees between $25 and $200. For example, Minnesota has a one cent per gallon tax on all gasoline sold in the state, while North Dakota charges a flat annual fee of $125 per UST and $75 per above-ground tank. At the end of 1995, there were

---

[16] Shalowitz, Deborah, "EPA Cuts Coverage Rules for Underground Tanks," *Business Insurance*, October 31, 1988.

[17] General Accounting Office, *Hazardous Waste: An Update on the Cost and Availability of Pollution Insurance*, GAO, Washington, D.C., 1994, p. 13.

34 SGFs in place, although several of them were operating under enormous deficits.[18]

Insurability Conditions

The following discussion describes why environmental risks from leaking USTs match the conditions of insurability, and what specific conditions of insurability insurance meets in providing coverage.

Condition 1: Identifying the Risk

Using past data on UST leaks compiled from various studies, including specific federal regulations, it is possible to determine the percentage of tanks of various ages likely to leak and the expected cost of cleanup and tank replacement. These data enable the insurer to estimate loss frequency and average loss with respect to the magnitude of the losses.

The University of Tennessee conducted a study of total costs to clean up leaking USTs in the United States. In a survey of over 75,000 sites, estimated current average cost to clean up USTs is $175,000.[19] The study included third-party estimates for incidents of off-site migration with ensuing third-party lawsuits. Costs for this liability averaged $2.5 million to $5 million.[20]

Condition 2: Setting the Risk Premium

There is relatively little ambiguity regarding the probability of a specific UST leaking if one is able to identify the type of tank, its age, and the materials used in its construction. The magnitude of the loss is somewhat uncertain, but it can be estimated within a reasonable range.

By insisting on tank inspections prior to providing coverage, insurers should be able to discriminate between good and bad risks and set the premiums accordingly. This eliminates the problem of adverse selection.

By requiring monitoring devices on tanks, insurers can detect leaks early and avoid large cleanup expenses. Insured businesses have no incentive to behave carelessly because they know the insurer will detect a leak as soon as it occurs. The use of deductibles, coinsurance, and upper limits on a policy also discourages behavior that could increase the chances of a loss. Hence, there does not appear to be a moral hazard problem.

---

[18] Cowans, Deborah Shalowitz, "State Assurance Funds Faltering: Recent Developments Cast Doubt on Reliability of Funds," *Business Insurance*, October 2, 1995, pp. 1–21.

[19] University of Tennessee, Hazardous Waste Remediation Project. Waste Management Research and Education Institute, *Underground Storage Tanks: Resource Requirements for Corrective Action*, University of Tennessee, Knoxville, TN, December 1991. p. 88.

[20] Ibid. p. 57 (d).

Correlative risk is not an issue in underground tank risk, because each tank is an independent unit. Leakage from one tank will have no impact on others. The only issue regarding correlation of risk relates to any changes in the liability laws regarding the degree to which cleanup needs to occur. New rulings on "how clean is clean" would have an impact on the amount that insurers would have to pay on all tanks covered by a policy.

Marketability Issues

The original EPA framework for UST regulation provided an opportunity for private insurance and loss prevention techniques to be employed. The creation of State Guarantee Funds (SGFs), however, effectively eliminated the opportunity for use of private insurance coverage in those states with SGFs. As pointed out above, SGFs are usually funded by an indirect means of taxation, usually based on a per gallon charge on stored petroleum products, not on the risk of leakage. Revenues from many of these SGFs do not provide sufficient funds for cleanup expenses and must be supplemented through cross-subsidization[21] and funding from other tax sources.

Several state programs are now severely underfunded because of competing pressures to utilize tax dollars for other needs. In 1995, the EPA withdrew its approval of the Michigan and Illinois SGFs after these funds became insolvent.

To illustrate the problems facing SGFs, we will provide a brief history of the Michigan fund. The state legislature adopted the Michigan Underground Storage Tank Financial Assurance (MUSTFA) program in 1988. The program reimburses UST owners for remediating contaminated sites and making payments to injured third parties. In addition, the program subsidizes loans for the replacement of leaking tanks. A fee of 7/8 of a cent per gallon of refined petroleum sold finances the program.

An audit of the MUSTFA program in 1993 found that, during the first two years of the program, total revenues were slightly less than $110 million and expenditures were approximately $250 million. A more detailed analysis of the program in 1995 projected that the existing claims would exceed available reserves by between $85 and $235 million dollars. MUSTFA has subsequently announced that it has stopped accepting claims because the fund is insolvent. It lost a court battle with the Michigan Petroleum Marketers Association, however, and is now under court order to continue accepting claims, even though it cannot afford to pay for them.[22] By the end of 1995, the program had a deficit of approximately $50 million.[23]

SGFs spend a greater percentage of their funds on administration and fees than they do on cleanup. Of the $4 million MUSTFA collects monthly, $2.5 million goes

---

[21] Villani, John, Daniel E. Ingberman and Howard Kunreuther, "The Development of Underground Storage Tank Regulations," Wharton Risk and Decision Processes Center, University of Pennsylvania, Philadelphia, July 31, 1991.

[22] Cowans, Deborah Shalowitz, "State Assurance Funds Faltering: Recent Developments Cast Doubt on Reliability of Funds," *Business Insurance*, October 2, 1995, pp. 1–21.

[23] Ibid. MUSTFA approved $67 million in payments by August 31, 1995, but is only able to pay approximately $1.5 million per month.

to pay for debt service and administrative fees. Illinois is in the same situation, expending 60 percent of its monthly income on bonds it bought to keep the program alive.[24]

Since funds are not available for cleanup, some contamination often remains in the ground for years. Some states are once again examining the role that private insurers can play in either supplementing (Florida) or replacing (Iowa) existing SGF programs. Some states are considering dismantling their programs altogether. In a *Business Insurance* article, Bill Child of the Illinois EPA said, "We - the Illinois Environmental Protection Agency - would like to get out of the fund business."[25]

However, it is possible that the SGFs still have a valuable role to play in conjunction with private insurance. It has been suggested that SGFs and private insurance together can encourage efficient UST management.[26] SGFs ideally handle coverage of retroactive environmental problems, while private insurance best meets RCRA's prospective financial responsibility requirements. More specifically, each state's UST program should offer amnesty from the costs of existing contamination up to some specified date. Thus the SGF would finance the cleanup of historic contamination and provide an incentive for the timely discovery and reporting of environmental problems. Beyond that date, the tank owner would be liable and subject to financial responsibility requirements.

Under this proposed system there is an incentive for private insurers to enter the market and to provide prospective coverage against future leaks. Currently, however, the cost of SGF coverage is much lower than the premiums private insurers would have to charge.[27]

The situation is ripe for change, since almost all SGFs are experiencing financial difficulty. UST owners have been advised to seek other sources of coverage in order to comply with RCRA's financial responsibility requirements.[28] One of these options is private insurance.

There are a number of variations on the type of private insurance systems available. New Jersey, for instance, currently has no SGF, so private insurance is the only option for businesses with insufficient assets to self-insure. The State of Washington requires tank owners to obtain private insurance or self-insure for the first $75,000 of coverage, while the state covers the balance. Also, UST owners must conduct an environmental assessment to determine if releases have occurred as a precondition to qualify for the program. Several states' SGFs, e.g., Maryland, Michigan, Minnesota, and Ohio, have deductibles that mimic a common feature of private insurance. Each state needs to consider how to use private insurance to supplement or replace its existing program.

---

[24] Ibid.

[25] Ibid.

[26] Boyd, James and Howard Kunreuther, "Retroactive Liability and Future Risk: The Optimal Regulation of Underground Storage Tanks," *Wharton Risk Management and Decision Processes Center Working Paper*, Wharton School, University of Pennsylvania, Philadelphia, PA, September 1995.

[27] In numerous states, SGFs are financed through taxes on gasoline. In this case, the cost of coverage to UST owners is effectively zero.

[28] See "UST Funds," *Environmental Alert Bulletin*, June 1995, p. 2.

In lieu of a private insurance market, it is desirable to have SGFs adopt the safeguards used by private insurers to limit moral hazard and adverse selection problems — deductibles, co-payments, and the denial of coverage for failure to meet technical standards. Since the SGF program, like most government benefit programs, relies on *ex post* remedies, little emphasis on *ex ante* loss prevention techniques occurs, even though UST regulations prescribe these measures. Emphasis on tank monitoring, inspection, and replacement reduces the ultimate damage and cost to society.

Summary and Conclusions

Congress and the EPA attempted to provide a comprehensive program to minimize damage from UST leakage and subsequent soil and groundwater contamination. Regulations were well-specified and clear, requiring financial assurance. Thus, private insurers began developing coverages based upon the risk characteristics of the tanks.

The failure of the private market to effectively play a role in the UST market is the direct result of the government's creation of an alternative market through the use of SGFs. Since these funds based their rates on criteria not correlated with the actual risk, they tended to undercharge for the risk. The ability of commercial entities to meet their financial responsibility requirements by using these underfunded SGFs effectively eliminated private insurance from the UST insurance marketplace.

As SGFs have evolved over the past few years, however, the willingness of states to cross-subsidize UST owners has diminished. Over the same period, unfortunately, the ultimate cost of remediation has been higher than it would have been if proper loss controls had been initiated earlier. Consequently, the ultimate cost to society of resolving the harm associated with USTs has also been higher than it needed to be.

III. LEAD-BASED PAINT

Lead has been used by metallurgists beginning as early as 3,000 B.C. Its low melting point, ductility, malleability, and durability were all desirable properties for many applications.

Lead occupies an important position in the U.S. economy, with an annual consumption of one million tons each year. The Occupational Safety and Health Administration (OSHA) has identified over 120 occupations in which workers may be exposed to lead. These include workers involved in the smelting industry, lead storage battery manufacturing, lead pigments use and manufacturing, solder manufacturing, ship building and repairing, auto manufacturing, and printing.

Lead has been used in paint pigments to provide corrosion and weather resistance and to enhance drying. Lead-based paints can contain up to 50 percent lead by weight.

Overview of the Risks

Beginning in the late 1960s, scientists discovered lead's potentially adverse health effects, especially on the central nervous system of young children. Exposure to lead can affect almost all of the body's systems. The early effects of lead poisoning are non-specific, and symptoms often become confused with those of the flu. The symptoms can include weakness, fatigue, sleep disturbance, headache, aching bones and muscles, digestive symptoms, abdominal pains, and decreased appetite. With continued exposure, symptoms include confusion with decreased alertness, anemia, pallor, and decreased hand-grip strength. If exposure continues, irreversible kidney damage may result.[29]

Children seem to absorb lead more readily than adults and the effects appear more drastically because of children's continuing bodily development. Symptoms in children include reduction of intelligence, alteration in behavior, poor attention span, and visual motor deficits. The neuropsychological problems detected in children have appeared with blood lead levels as low as 30 micrograms of lead per deciliter of blood (g/dl) or lower.

The major sources of exposure to inorganic lead are inhalation and ingestion. Larger lead particles inhaled generally deposit in the upper respiratory tract. From there, the lead moves to the gastrointestinal tract through ciliary action and swallowing. The very small lead particles may deposit in the lower respiratory tract, where they are absorbed directly and almost completely. This makes exposure to lead fumes a much greater exposure hazard.

The primary mechanism of exposure in young children is through ingesting lead-bearing dust. The source of the dust is, most commonly, deteriorating and flaking paint. Occupational exposure in lead-based paint abatement is highest from burning or heat removal and abrasive methods such as sanding, scraping, and bead blasting. Elevated airborne lead concentrations also appear during caustic stripping operations and when lead-painted components are being removed. Any risk assessment would have to utilize this exposure scenario. Procedures would have to be standardized through regulatory mandate, and permissible exposure levels established and enforced.

Traditional methods of abatement remained concerned only with the removal of peeling and flaking paint readily accessible to young children. Very little attempt was made to control or eliminate the pre-existing lead-bearing dust or the dust that resulted from the abatement procedures. There was typically no attempt to protect or

---

[29] United States Environmental Protection Agency, Office of Prevention, Pesticides and Toxic Substances, "EPA Proposes National Training, Certification, Accreditation and Standards Programs for Individuals and Firms Engaged in Lead-Based Paint Activities," *Environmental Fact Sheet*, September 1994, p. 1, "Health Effects of Lead."

cover family belongings. Cleanup procedures usually involved dry sweeping or using unfiltered vacuum cleaners. These techniques only served to re-deposit the lead-
bearing dust. The result was that the dwelling was no safer after the abatement took
place than before.

Abatement methods considered to be "state of the art," aimed at minimizing the
dust generated in the abatement process, prevent that dust from contaminating adja-
cent spaces. In this regard, the methods approximate those involved in doing asbestos abatement. Procedures include reducing airborne particles of lead dust, as
well as isolating the work site.

Regulatory Environment

In September 1977, the U. S. Consumer Product Safety commission banned the sale
of residential paints containing lead additives (in interstate commerce). However,
the 1980 U. S. Housing Census indicated that there were 27 million housing units
still occupied, built prior to 1940 when lead carbonate was the predominant white
pigment in house paints.

United States Department of Housing and Urban Development's (HUD) 1990
estimate, based on a study of private U. S. housing, indicated that as many as 13.8
million housing units contained chipping and peeling lead-based paint.[30] HUD estimated that there were approximately 57 million homes in the U. S. built prior to
1978 that contained lead-based paint.[31] The 1991 American Housing Survey (AHS)
found 6.2 million homes in poor physical condition: deteriorated and dilapidated,
with holes in the walls, peeling paint, and/or broken and cracked plaster.[32]

While the Third National Health and Nutrition Examination Survey (NHANES
III) reported, after completion of its first research phase, that blood lead levels in the
overall population had dropped dramatically over the past 15 years,[33] it has been
estimated that 1.7 million children from ages one to five have blood lead levels of
10 g/dl or higher.[34] The report of HUD's Task Force on the issue, described below,
contains additional information on the scope of lead poisoning in the U. S.[35]

---

[30] United States Department of Housing and Urban Development, *Comprehensive and Workable Plan
for the Abatement of Lead-Based Paint in Privately Owned Housing: Report to Congress*, Office of
Policy Development and Research, Washington, DC, December 7, 1990.

[31] United States Department of Housing and Urban Development, Task Force on Lead-Based Paint Hazard Reduction and Financing, *Putting the Pieces Together: Controlling Lead Hazards in the Nation's
Housing. Report*, (HUD-1547–LBP), July 1995, p. 36.

[32] United States Department of Commerce and Department of Housing and Urban Development, *1991
American Housing Survey*, Washington, DC, 1991.

[33] Pirkle, J.L. et al., "The Decline of Blood Lead Levels in the United States," *Journal of the American
Medical Association*, July 27, 1994, pp. 284–291.

[34] Brody, D.J., et al., "Blood Lead Levels in the U.S. Population," *Journal of the American Medical Association*, July 27, 1994, pp. 277–283.

[35] United States Department of Housing and Urban Development, Task Force on Lead-Based Paint Hazard Reduction and Financing, *Putting the Pieces Together: Controlling Lead Hazards in the Nation's
Housing, Report*, (HUD-1547–LBP), July, 1995.

Actions taken by HUD

The history of lead-based paint regulation dates back to 1971 when Congress passed the Lead-Based Paint Poisoning Prevention Act and directed HUD to establish procedures to eliminate lead poisoning as far as practical from HUD housing constructed prior to 1950. At a minimum, these procedures were to eliminate the immediate hazards to children and to notify purchasers and tenants of lead-based paint hazards, symptoms, treatment, and abatement techniques.

The Act was amended in February 1988 to include all HUD housing constructed or substantially modified prior to 1978. The amendment also extended the regulations to include essentially all painted surfaces within the dwelling, not only interior and exterior surfaces up to five feet from the floor or ground as specified in the original legislation.[36] Regulations called for a complete inspection of all HUD housing constructed prior to 1978 whenever a comprehensive modification and rehabilitation takes place, or when a child living in the unit is found to have elevated blood lead levels. The regulations also specify approved abatement methods. These include permanently attached coverings, such as wallboard and plywood, removal of paint, and replacement of components. Power sanding and open flame burning, which can release a large amount of lead fume into the air, are prohibited. The regulations also stipulate a number of additional safety measures, similar to those for asbestos removal:

1. Access to the work area is limited to personnel directly involved with the abatement.

2. The area is to be regulated through signs, barrier tape, and other security measures.

3. Movable objects, such as furniture, should be removed from the work area.

4. Stationary objects and other surfaces not to be abated should be covered with plastic sheeting to prevent contamination.

5. Clean up procedures following abatement should include wet wiping and high efficiency particulate filter (HEPA) vacuuming of all surfaces.

6. As the contaminant is in the form of a particulate, the work area should be placed under negative pressure and the ventilated air should be filtered through HEPA filters.

7. Personnel leaving the work area should not wear contaminated clothing outside and should shower when leaving.

---

[36] The regulations HUD issued in response to this Act are in 24 C. F. R. Part 35.

The regulations established in June 1988 were suspended pending completion of a set of guidelines from the National Institute of Building Sciences (NIBS) and a lead-based paint abatement demonstration project. The NIBS guidelines contain a survey of existing testing and abatement methods, which HUD received in February 1989. Since then, HUD established a "Task Force on Lead-Based Paint Hazard Reduction and Financing." In June 1995, the Task Force produced a document reporting its recommendations, entitled "Putting the Pieces Together: Controlling Lead Hazards in the Nation's Housing."[37]

The problem overview section of the executive summary notes that "Changes are needed in virtually every aspect of the nation's approach to lead-based paint hazards," and among these is the recognition that "the tort system is operating inefficiently and randomly for lead poisoning claims."[38]

The Task Force report proposed benchmark national standards for controlling lead hazards in private housing. According to the HUD press release from July 11, 1995, the benchmark standards are the first ever. Chapter three of the report outlines these standards. An item explaining the benefits of establishing benchmark standards reads:

> Benchmark standards provide a basis for insurers to underwrite lead-based paint liability coverage for owners of rental housing. If property owners follow standards and the legal system recognizes these standards as establishing the steps a reasonable property owner should take, liability risks would become predictable and insurable.[39]

The Task Force recognizes that current regulations are simply too vague to allow underwriting guidelines or accurate premium rates to be developed. They recognize, furthermore, that the tort liability system is not providing efficient or equitable compensation.[40]

The report advocates the creation of additional funding mechanisms for compensating children who become poisoned. A state sponsored, no-fault, remedial compensation plan was recommended to compensate children who were poisoned despite their landlord's compliance with the regulations. In addition, the report advocates a fund for those who might otherwise fall through the cracks. Landlords who do not have the resources to finance insurance, and families who have no health insurance, are among the groups who would benefit from this program.

These State-run programs would be funded by some type of taxation or surcharge. These proposed programs contain the same possibility of failure as the state UST solution. If states set up a general insurance fund too broad in scope, as with USTs, lead-based paint risks could be non-insurable. New regulations have yet to be promulgated, however, and further study and debate can be expected before any such action does occur.

---

[37] United States Department of Housing and Urban Development, Task Force on Lead-Based Paint Hazard Reduction and Financing, *Putting the Pieces Together: Controlling Lead Hazards in the Nation's Housing, Report,* (HUD-1547–LBP), July 1995.

[38] Ibid., p. 3.

[39] Ibid., p. 60.

[40] Ibid., p. 111.

Actions taken by OSHA

There currently are no OSHA regulations directly applicable to lead-based paint abatement. The construction standard for dusts, mists, and fumes sets a Threshold Limit Value[41] for airborne lead concentrations at 200 g/m^3. OSHA has promulgated regulations for lead in general industry[42] establishing Permissible Exposure Limits (PEL) at 50 g/m^3 and action levels at 30 g/m^3. The action level triggers requirements aimed at preventing further harmful exposure. They also call for employee notification and training, exposure monitoring, medical surveillance, use of engineering and administrative controls, and use of personal protective equipment, including respirators and full body coveralls. The regulations specify that workers shall not wear contaminated clothing out of the work area and that they should shower before leaving the work area.

OSHA published an interim final rule on "Lead Exposure in Construction" in the Federal Register[43] that has not yet made it to final form.[44] The rule proposes to reduce permissible exposure levels and set standards for work practices, methods of compliance, worker safety, and other items. In short, the rule would provide additional regulatory specificity where it is currently lacking.

Actions taken by the EPA

The Environmental Protection Agency has also proposed rules for lead-based paint mandated under the Toxic Substances Control Act. Published as "Lead; Requirements for Lead-Based Paint Activities; Proposed Rule" in the Federal Register[45], the rules[46] primarily regulate workers engaged in lead-based paint activities. These regulations mandate that such workers receive proper training and certification to perform their work, and require the accreditation of training programs. This rule is also not yet in final form.

Insurability Conditions

In contrast to asbestos abatement, the regulatory environment for lead-based paint abatement is not well established. Recent attempts to improve the situation may aid insurability, but the historical situation has made it very difficult.

The OSHA regulations promulgated thus far for lead in general industry do not apply to construction or abatement. No EPA regulations have yet been enacted. Current HUD regulations provide minimal guidance. They prohibit certain methods of abatement, but fall short of requiring proper engineering controls and industrial hygiene procedures to minimize the spread of lead contamination outside the work

---

[41] 29 C. F. R. Part 1926.55
[42] 29 C. F. R. Part 1910.1025
[43] 59 Fed. Reg. 170.
[44] The rule involves the addition of section 62 to 29 C. F. R. Part 1926.
[45] 58 Fed. Reg. 84.
[46] Final form would be promulgated as 40 C. F. R. Part 745.

area. Since all of these regulations are unenforceable outside their limited jurisdictions, they can only be considered as a guide for reasonable and prudent action and not as a means of enforcing behavior.

Without clear regulatory guidelines, the insurability of lead-based paint remediation is problematic at best. First, establishing rates for coverage is difficult because the level of permissible exposure is not well specified, and is subject to change. Therefore, modeling must assume worst case exposure levels as the basis for actuarial rate determination.

It is unlikely that insurance providers could design lead-based paint abatement coverage that would be attractive to enough potential insureds to make it a profitable product. In the absence of reliable information on permissible exposure levels, insurance providers must impose standards in excess of those required by government regulation. Historically, this procedure has resulted in failure. Insureds in competitive building industries in particular are unwilling to adhere to standards that increase their costs when competitors are not equally constrained.

Some insurers have been able to provide limited coverage for lead-based paint remediation activities for contractors who currently perform asbestos remediation. In place of regulatory enforcement, insurers have required proof of safe work practices in asbestos abatement, and certified training in lead-based paint abatement and safety procedures.

Summary and Conclusions

Lead is a pervasive health hazard widely used in a variety of materials. The primary health risk to society comes from lead used in paints that are applied to residential dwellings. The primary method of lead poisoning is through inhalation of lead dust or ingestion of dust or paint particles. Children are especially susceptible to the negative effects of lead on their developing nervous systems, and are more likely to accidentally poison themselves through normal hand-to-mouth behavior.

Risks associated with lead-based paint occur mainly in residential dwellings where deteriorating paint inhaled as dust or ingested by children as dust or paint chips poisons the children. There are also significant risks associated with lead-based paint removal. If improper removal occurs, it either has no positive effect or increases the risk of exposure.

Insuring against these risks is extremely difficult since the regulations surrounding lead exposure and removal are confusing and poorly specified. Liabilities implied by regulations are unclear, and standards for exposure do not adequately specify permissible levels. There is also the likelihood that regulations will soon change, given the level of activity and debate over the issue. These shortcomings make the development of private insurance coverage difficult because of the inability to identify or quantify the risk precisely. Premiums would have to be based on worst case scenarios and there are likely to be too few potential buyers to make the coverage profitable for any firm.

Some coverage is available in connection with asbestos remediation, however. Recent attempts by the regulatory agencies (HUD, OSHA, and EPA) to deal with these issues are moving in the right direction by attempting to develop and enforce standards at the national levels.

IV. LESSONS FOR INSURANCE AND RISK MANAGEMENT

The above three examples of environmental risks offer some guidance on ways that society can better manage its risks in the future through the insurance mechanism. Generally, for insurance to succeed there needs to be well-specified standards or regulations that help delineate the risk. This will enable the proposed product to meet the conditions of insurability.

As we have seen, however, this is only one part of the story. For insurance to be a marketable product there also must be sufficient demand at a premium which covers product development and administrative costs, including sales and distribution expenses for the product.

Environmentally Contaminated Property

The analysis of data on environmental contamination suggests the importance of third-party inspections through audits or site assessments as a precondition for insurance. These inspections reduce the ambiguity associated with the probability that there is contamination on the land. If an audit suggests that the proposed building site is clean, there is still some chance that contamination exists. This estimate of the probability of damage, coupled with a distribution of loss estimates, enables the insurer to set a premium that reflects the risk. The principal ambiguity associated with the risk is the cost that will have be incurred should contamination be found. To the extent that there is a well-specified standard as to "how clean is clean," which currently doesn't exist, the insurer can be more confident about the nature of the risk and the premium.

Should contamination be detected through the site assessment process, the current owner has a chance to clean it up before selling the property. Such action will be taken if the expected benefits from selling the property exceed the seller's expected cleanup cost. For parcels of land where this is desirable, the site assessment may facilitate the cleanup of the nation's hazardous waste in ways that go beyond the standard process.

With respect to the demand for this type of insurance, data are available. Marketing experience since the product was introduced in 1992 suggests that most property owners will not voluntarily purchase coverage as contractors now do for asbestos abatement protection. Owners either believe that a site assessment is sufficient or feel that remediation costs would be relatively low should contamination be found on the land.

There is a potential solution to this lack of interest in buying insurance. One can include insurance as part of a larger package so that it is relatively inexpensive in the context of the transaction. In addition, if banks require this coverage, then demand will soar and be viewed by the property owners as relatively painless. Lessons from the title insurance arena may be instructive here. Title insurance, normally required by lenders, would be viewed as somewhat expensive if not bundled with the rest of the real estate transaction. When combined with the costs of settling the property, however, it appears to be a marginal additional expense.

Underground Storage Tanks (USTs)

With respect to USTs, there are a well-specified set of regulations and cost data that define the expected losses associated with a leaky tank. Hence, the risks from these tanks are considered insurable. Financial responsibility requirements imposed on tank owners by RCRA appeared to be an ideal way to encourage these businesses to purchase insurance coverage.

The demand for coverage never materialized, however, because small businesses convinced many state legislatures to create State Guarantee Funds either by assessing a flat fee on all USTs and/or by levying a tax per gallon of fuel sold. These SGFs satisfied the EPA's FRR requirements imposed by RCRA. This solution undermined the motivation of the market to purchase private insurance, since the taxes and fees were levied on all tank owners, independent of their risk and whether or not they had other types of coverage.

The most unfortunate consequence of this development is that there is little incentive for tank owners to undertake preventive measures or inspect their tanks if the SGFs will cover both past and future leaks. A more desirable policy would be to have SGFs cover historic contamination if the firm agrees to upgrade its tanks, and use private insurance to cover future liabilities. This does not discourage UST owners and operators from undertaking future risk reduction measures such as upgrading a tank system.

The case for private insurance can be made even stronger given the insolvency of several SGFs. In particular, Michigan and Illinois have expended such large sums of money on both administering the fund and paying out claims that the EPA no longer recognizes these state's funds as meeting their FRR. Hence, there may be a market for private insurance emerging in the near future.

Lead-Based Paint

Lead used in paint is a health hazard, especially to young children. Even though experts have identified lead as a hazard since at least the late 1960s, regulations for the removal and control of lead-based paint in residential and commercial facilities are still poorly specified.

While attempts have been made recently to remedy this situation, unclear liabilities and standards have prevented private insurers from developing policies. Coverage must be based upon enforced standards, such as permissible exposure levels.

Otherwise pricing must rely on worst case scenarios that may lead to such high premiums that there will be limited market demand. According to HUD's Task Force, lack of coverage for these risks also has hindered the financing of cleanup and compensation of the injured.

Conclusions

Environmental insurance can work well as a cost-effective means to reduce societal risks, with the help of government regulations and private standards. We have seen how lack of some type of requirement impairs the marketability of insurance (Property Transfer Coverage). We have also seen how state attempts to replace insurance through funding mechanisms have failed (USTs). Finally, we have seen that unclear specification and enforcement of environmental standards leave unpredictable risks that are uninsurable (Lead-based Paint).

It therefore becomes clear that development of government regulation ought to take into account the needs of private insurers to develop and market new products. If insurance encourages loss prevention measures and provides compensation to those who suffer losses, then it is likely to meet a set of society's needs. Such a partnership between the private and public sectors will yield dividends to all the interested parties—the public at risk, industrial firms, insurers, and government agencies.

8

SUMMARY AND
CONCLUSIONS

Part I of this book began with an examination of the three principal ways that our nation manages societal risk, namely through: (1) government benefit programs, (2) the legal system, and (3) private insurance. Each risk transfer method has its own set of characteristics.

As indicated in Chapter 1, government benefit programs focus on equity, or fairness, over efficiency; evaluate claimants after a loss occurs (*ex post* evaluation); have low administrative costs; and compete for funding with all other government programs during the budgeting process. The legal system, on the other hand, seeks to compensate injured parties and to deter others from engaging in similar activities, but, as detailed in Chapter 2, at a cost that can be very high. Chapter 3 concluded that, in light of these shortcomings, private insurance provides better cost efficiency, spreads risk across larger groups, reduces the variance of the risk, discriminates between different classes of potential insureds, encourages loss reduction measures as a condition of insurance, and monitors the activities of insureds.

It is clear from this examination that insurance has been, and continues to be, a powerful tool for managing societal risk in general. When the subject is narrowed to managing environmental risk, as indicated in Part II of this book, it is also clear that insurance can offer major advantages over government benefit programs and the legal system in this specific area as well.

Compared to government benefit programs, insurance provides a private sector solution that avoids the creation of more government bureaucracy and, in addition, requires risk reduction activities as a condition of coverage. Compared to the legal system, insurance can provide greater compensation to injured parties than costly litigation is able to provide. Chapters 5 and 6 detailed how coverage was successfully developed and marketed for the removal of asbestos in existing properties and, to a lesser extent, for properties with asbestos in place. These chapters also illustrated the ability to develop coverage for property to be transferred where there may be environmental contamination.

But, as noted in Chapter 4, insurance is no "magic bullet" for the effective and efficient management, and prevention, of environmental risk. As indicated throughout Part II, insurance coverage cannot be developed for every type of environmental risk.

For example, coverage could not be developed for underground storage tanks and lead-based paint removal.

It is critical that leaders in both the public and private sectors understand the benefits of insurance, and its limitations, if insurance is to be more broadly applied in the future to the management of environmental risk. We summarize those benefits and limitations in this concluding chapter.

I. BENEFITS

The benefits of insurance flow from its distinctive characteristics as a tool to spread risk across a broad spectrum of risk bearers. These characteristics can be grouped under five major headings: specialization of the industry, risk prevention mechanisms, focus on risk reduction, lack of cross-subsidization, and lower delivery cost.

Specialization of the Industry

The insurance industry can ideally assume many types of societal risk. With a profit motivation, insurance firms calculate the cost of risk of an event, and collect premiums to cover losses from pre-specified events. By assuming risks in this way, insurance has evolved into a business with built-in resources for specialized information processing, complex statistical calculation, scientific and legal research and product marketing and distribution.

The payment of losses through risk-based insurance policies is self-funded from premiums received. This makes insurance a reliable financial mechanism for funding risk, because insurance specializes in reserving (and investing) collected funds for the purpose of claims payment. As a result, insurance is more likely to have funds to cover losses over time than government subsidized programs, which have to compete for funding with other government programs that are subject to changes in political climate. Consider the example of state government-created underground storage tank programs discussed in Chapter 7. Many of these programs failed, or are failing, due to lack of funding, as summarized in this news release from the Illinois EPA:

> There is approximately $300,000 available per month from the motor fuel tax to pay [leaking underground storage tank] claims.

> The backlog status as of September 25, 1995 is:

1,200 sites waiting for payment;

$44 million owed to tank owners and operators;

12 1/2 years to pay it all.[1]

Risk Prevention Mechanisms

Insurance, unlike the legal system or government programs, requires, and provides incentives for, *ex ante* loss prevention. Since the tort system essentially acts as a deterrent and compensation mechanism for injury, payments are made only after damage has occurred. Government programs, likewise, make no demands on claimants to alter their behavior or employ risk reduction techniques in order to qualify for benefits. These programs simply ascertain if claimants qualify for damages and then pays them. Thus, both systems employ *ex post* funding mechanisms.

Ex ante prevention systems have the desired benefit of reducing overall risk. Insurance provides incentives and requirements to prevent losses. The cost and availability of insurance is often linked to specific risk prevention measures, as described in Chapter 3, thereby motivating customers to comply. Application requirements and continuous monitoring tend to improve compliance with established safety standards.

As seen in the case of underground storage tanks in Chapter 7, the lack of standards can actually increase the likelihood of an adverse event. Since tank owners did not monitor tanks for leaks in order to qualify for funds to clean up any contamination caused by their leaking tanks, more tanks leaked than if monitoring devices were in place.

Focus on Risk Reduction

Economy of scale benefits flow from insurers' use of the law of large numbers to spread exposure across a large population. As described in Chapter 3, an increase in the size of the sample of uncorrelated risks improves the certainty of loss frequency and loss severity estimates. Every purchaser of an insurance policy contributes a small share in order to avoid a severe loss in the event of a catastrophe. By spreading risk across a broad group, insurance reduces an individual's risk of a large loss and reduces the variance for the group as a whole by application of the law of large numbers.

---

[1] Illinois Environmental Protection Agency, "UST Fund Overwhelmed by Payment Claims," *The LUST Release*, State of Illinois, Fall 1995, p. 4 (back cover).

Lack of Cross-subsidization

The use of insurance reduces subsidization of risk by unaffected individuals or businesses. By calculating the probability associated with described, definable categories of risk, insurers set a premium that accurately reflects each risk. As a result, individuals who purchase coverage against a particular event are paying premiums that should correlate with the frequency and magnitude of that potential loss. Those not exposed to the risk do not subsidize those who face a potential loss. Chapters 3 and 4 describe this effect. The example of UST state funds in Chapter 7 illustrates how all drivers in a state subsidize, in part, tank owners in that state through taxes paid on all gasoline purchases.

Government benefit programs do not discriminate between risks, nor between individuals engaging in different types of activities or residing in different locations. For example, all taxpayers help pay for some of the relief provided to natural disaster victims who live in high-risk geographic locations.[2]

Cross-subsidization can have important public policy implications. In times of fiscal restraint, the public is likely to look less favorably on government benefit programs that subsidize some individuals and businesses at the expense of all taxpayers.

Lower Delivery Cost

When compared with the current tort liability system, insurance delivers a greater percentage of collected funds to cleanup or compensation. Chapter 2 showed the average fund distribution for delivering compensation to asbestos injury claimants through the tort liability system was approximately 40 percent of total funds collected. By contrast, in Chapter 3 we saw that the average amount available to claimants from insurance was approximately 66 cents of every premium dollar collected.

The studies of UST funds suggest that insurance is also likely to be more efficient than government benefit programs. The underfunding of UST state funds, and the expenditure of a significant portion of funds to pay debt servicing, make the delivery of cleanup funds from UST state funds just as costly as the tort system. Insurance provides better risk management for less.

II. LIMITATIONS

Despite having the potential to be a powerful tool for dealing with societal risk, insurance has qualities that can limit its applicability and effectiveness. For example,

---

[2] Priest, George L., "The Government, the Market and the Problem of Catastrophic Loss," *Conference on Social Treatment of Catastrophic Risk: Stanford University - Lucas Conference Center*, October 21, 1994, pp. 29–32.

insurance values efficiency over equity, works best with limited types of risks, and must be marketable in order be effective.

Values Efficiency Over Equity

Unlike government benefit programs, insurers must be able to discriminate between groups of insureds to be effective. Government benefit programs in the United States compensate individuals as uniformly as possible, despite varying risk profiles—as illustrated by UST owners/operators and natural catastrophe victims.

The subsidization of UST owners and victims of flood or earthquake by all taxpayers is the direct result of a uniform compensation approach that does not discriminate among risks. Insurance, by way of contrast, charges higher premiums to those who have higher risk profiles, and does not insure some risks at all. As a result, there are likely to be fewer individuals exposed to risks covered under insurance than under government benefit programs.

If a loss has already occurred without insurance in place, as in the cases asbestos injury and identified contamination, then insurers cannot normally provide an insurance policy. In other words, insurance does not normally apply to known events.[3] The tort system is better at providing *ex post* punishment and compensation in such situations.

Limited to Insurable Risks

Insurance can only be applied to societal risks that are insurable. More specifically, understanding and quantifying a risk is necessary in order to develop a premium which reflects the expected losses.

As shown in the asbestos example in Chapters 5 and 6, government regulations are often instrumental in reducing the ambiguity of a risk, because they set standards of behavior. This is a key step in making a risk measurable, because it serves as a foundation for the development of a "breakeven" premium. Well-defined regulations yield predictable losses, and insurance works best with predictable losses.

Losses are predictable across potential insureds when the government maintains a level playing field, enforcing the same standards on all regulated companies. As a result, firms are more likely to voluntarily purchase insurance than they would be if they were unsure of whether a particular standard would be imposed and enforced.

---

[3] The one exception is if there is uncertainty as to when a payment will be made for an event that has already occurred. For example, insurance was provided after the MGM Grand Fire occurred on how long it would take to settle the claim.

Marketability: Tickle, Trigger, Hammer

Since, insurance only works when it is purchased, conditions under which insurance will sell require attention. Entities may be influenced to purchase insurance by a range of government or market activities. The range of motivating forces, sometimes called "tickle, trigger or hammer," provides purchase incentives at a variety of levels.

A "tickle" pressure may be a preference that encourages insurance purchase, such as optional insurance provisions requested by a property owner from contractors working on a project. This may be a request for higher limits of liability to be made available to the owner by the contractor. Tickle pressure may also take the form of a promise of greater profits in the marketplace. For example, a product indirectly guaranteed by product liability insurance may have greater market appeal and generate higher sales than one that does not carry this insurance.

"Triggering" involves motivating an insurance purchase as one means of covering a potential risk. For example, a bank may permit its customers to either insure a risk, or to place a deposit with the bank to cover the potential, unknown exposure. Often, insurance is the preferred option.

"Hammering" is "requiring" insurance as a virtual "license to operate," often with strict penalties for non-compliance. This is the most effective means of marketing insurance. Asbestos abatement project owners typically require remediation contractors to carry asbestos liability insurance to protect themselves from liabilities that could stem from the contractor's work. Since a contractor without insurance is unlikely to secure work, he or she has a strong incentive to purchase insurance.

However, if government takes "hammering" too far, it places the insurer in the role of government enforcer. When government rules stipulate that compliance with insurance equals compliance with the law, the insurer may assume a level of responsibility that is inconsistent with its risk bearing role. The International Chamber of Commerce has adopted the following view:

> Compulsory financial security instruments as a condition for obtaining a license to carry out certain activities or handle certain substances would pose immense difficulties. In such circumstances, compulsory insurance could result in insurers, in effect, becoming regulators.[4]

If the insurer makes an error in monitoring or compliance enforcement, it becomes directly liable. This situation changes policy by transferring legal liability from the target regulated group to the insurance company. This situation changes the focus of the government regulation, and it also fundamentally alters the insurer/insured relationship. The insurer would become, in effect, a watchdog over its customers rather than a service provider.

Besides the influence of government on insurance, other market factors may limit its effectiveness as well. Insurance appeals more to certain types of businesses

---

[4] "Environmental Liability and Financial Security," *Position Paper: Adopted in October 1993*, International Chamber of Commerce, Commission on Insurance, October 1993, p. 4.

than to others. Small and medium-sized firms with annual revenues of less than $100 million are the primary purchasers of coverage. Firms with annual revenues greater than $5 billion are far more likely to self-insure their exposures. So, while insurance has many benefits, it also has its limitations with regard to the conditions under which it is most effective.

III. CONCLUSION

As a social policy tool, insurance is a powerful instrument. The ability to quantify, control, and transfer risk has been an important feature of insurance since its inception. With respect to certain environmental risks, insurance can provide substantial benefits over the tort legal system through a reduction in transaction costs. Unlike government benefit programs, insurance encourages loss prevention and avoids cross-subsidization.

But, insurance has its limitations. In order to work effectively and efficiently, insurance must be allowed to discriminate between risks. It cannot be expected to cover all risks. Insurance also must have enough market appeal to be purchased (preferably voluntarily) if it is to work. To date, there are only a few environmental risks which satisfy these conditions.

This book has attempted to show the conditions under which insurance can operate as a viable risk reduction tool in the environmental arena. When environmental risks are defined by well-specified standards of behavior, when costs are predictable, and when individuals and businesses are motivated to purchase coverage, insurance can ease the potential consequences of loss in a cost-effective and efficient manner that reduces uncertainty. We hope this discussion will foster the more widespread use of insurance for the successful management of well-defined environmental risks.

INDEX

www.ingramcontent.com/pod-product-compliance
Lightning Source LLC
Jackson TN
JSHW011351130125
77033JS00015B/559